MW01074061

Falling Out of Grace
Meditations on Loss, Healing and Wisdom

ALSO BY SOBONFU E. SOMÉ

Spirit of Intimacy:
Ancient Teachings in the Ways of Relationships

Welcoming Spirit Home:
Ancient African Teachings to Celebrate Children and Community

Falling Out of Grace
Meditations on Loss, Healing and Wisdom

By Sobonfu E. Somé

NORTH BAY BOOKS
EL SOBRANTE, CALIFORNIA

Published by
North Bay Books
P. O. Box 21234
El Sobrante, California 94820
(510) 758-4276
www.northbaybooks.com

Comments and inquiries regarding this book may also be sent to
john@northbaybooks.com

Copyright © 2003 Sobonfu E. Somé
All rights reserved, including the right of reproduction, in whole or
in part in any form.

Cover design by Elysium, San Francisco.
Printed by United Graphics, Mattoon, Illinois.
Distributed by Publishers Group West.

ISBN: 0-9725200-2-3
Library of Congress Control Number: 2003106800

First Printing: July, 2003

Table of Contents

Foreword

I first met Sobonfu Somé in the winter of 1991 in Ann Arbor, Michigan. It was a cold, gray, leafless, snow-dusted afternoon in southeast Michigan; how different from the remote village in Burkina Faso and the sun-baked West African summer she had left behind just a few months earlier.

Sobonfu had arrived in the United States to join her new husband, who was then teaching at the University of Michigan. Their apartment was filled with the smells of African cooking — bitters, sweets and pungents unlike any I had encountered before. The meal that followed, rich with colors and textures that rarely reach tables in the West, reflected a new culinary language. Sobonfu had not only prepared a selection of familiar flavors combined in surprising ways, but also offered a wholly new understanding of food: of its sources, of its purpose, and of how it needs to be cooked and served to please and nourish those who partake of it.

In the years since I have had the privilege of working with Sobonfu on a number of projects, and of her friendship. I have seen this pattern repeated throughout her relationships with Westerners. To those who discover her she brings gifts they are unlikely to receive from homegrown teachers, and these gifts show them new ways of thinking, seeing and acting, enabling them to live, at least in some small way, with the strength of greater awareness.

Sobonfu's story has been well told in her previous books, *The Spirit of Intimacy* and *Welcoming Spirit Home*: how her life purpose as "keeper of the rituals" was discovered while she was still in her mother's womb; how she was born into a small village of the Dagara people in rural West Africa; how she was raised in a world shaped and populated by Spirit, among people unaffected by the posturing and self-interest that characterize western culture; and how she continues to live in two worlds — one modern, one indigenous — living part of the year at home in Burkina Faso and part here in a sprawling American urban center.

This is a rare and beautiful story, but it is not the one told in this book. Although Sobonfu's life is unique in so many ways, she shares with all of us the human experiences of loss and disappointment, of being wounded by our own errors or the behavior of those around us. As she writes in her preface, since leaving the village she has "experienced many crashes," facing some of the most difficult personal challenges one meets with in life. This book is, in part, a Phoenix rising from the fires she has passed through. It was written in order to help readers understand the nature of "falling from grace," to show them that they are not alone in their experience of loss and failure, and to describe how these events function to our benefit as tools of Spirit.

Although this book addresses universal issues of learning and suffering, it does so in a way that perhaps no one could have written but Sobonfu. It comes from a place where modern and ancient, Western and African, rural and urban, communal and consumerist converge. It comes from a place where a rigorous education in the benevolent spiritual realities behind everyday life has been tested by the painful experiences we all face as we become adults. That is the place where Sobonfu lives. I am grateful to her for doing the hard work of analyzing the sources and purpose of our falls from grace, and then offering her knowledge to us through a book that so richly satisfies our hunger for greater wisdom.

John Strohmeier
Richmond, California

Gratitude

My respect and fondness to my family and village, whose unconditional love continues to make my imperfections bearable. I cannot thank you enough for breathing life into me and accepting me as I am.

My love to my nieces and nephews, who helped me to recognize the multiple layers and dimensions of my failures.

My deepest gratitude to my sister, angel and friend Susan Hough, whose love and belief in me made it possible for her to provide the means to produce this book.

My love and sincere gratitude to Diane Truly, who provided me with a place I could call home while I wrote.

My great respect and thank you to His Holiness Ajahn Jumnien, and to Jack and Liana Kornfield, for their prayers and wisdom. Thank you. It made all the difference in my life.

My regards to Linda Teixeira, who gave her time and love in transcribing. May your hands always bring healing.

My heartfelt appreciation to my loving friends: trees, lands, waters, rocks, Dieneba, Marcia Fitten and R.A.A., Michele Evans, Julia Ashton and family, Gioia Timpanelli, Mark Goodwin, Amina J., Kathy Bauers and friends in Colorado, Pat Morse, Ruth and Robert Bly, The Nine Gates Mystery School family, Lynn and Kevin, Mary Okocha, Le A. Perez, Damon Miller, Alice Walker, the Villagers, Mama Elaine, Kristina and the Mailliard family, Karen Mason, Connie

Kaplan, John Strohmeier, Laura Pérez and Maya, Adelia, the
Achords, Meg, Susan and Keith and family, Erica H. Meade,
Lyndal and Bayard Johnson, Toby and Michele, Emilio, Harriet
Wright, S. Arms, Gale Thompson, Ayeola, Chache Kalamu,
Laurie Casey, Debora C., John Scaife and Luli H., Marrow,
Don Morrison, Kadi Cisse, Leona, my Bay Area and Sacra-
mento friends, Laura McIntyre, Penny Ukadike, Babsy and
Ellen, and all those who stood by me while my world crumbled
into millions of pieces. You know who you are. Thanks for
loving and supporting me without judgements.

My gratitude also to those who have been awaiting the
appearance of this book. Your patience has made it possible
for me not to give birth to it prematurely.

My best wishes to all those who contributed to and created the perfect situations for me to fall from grace. Thank
you for opening new doorways for me to walk through.

This book is dedicated to my grandmother,
whose understanding of failure gave me
a sense of humor to maneuver through life;
and to my brother Minmin,
who enjoyed and celebrated each of his failures thoroughly.
May your spirits always ride with me.

Preface

I have been pregnant with this book for a long time. The idea grew out of a discussion I had with a friend, now more than six years ago, as we explored different ways of dealing with personal crises. The deeper we got into our subject, the more clearly I saw how difficult it is to address our failings and find ways to restore ourselves without considering the larger community, our professional lives, our spirituality, and so forth.

After an evening of pondering these related ideas, bringing to bear many of my own experiences related to home, relationships, work, and what I saw as my role in the world, my friend concluded, "Sobonfu, it sounds like you have fallen out of grace."

I wondered, at first, what in the world she meant by "falling out of grace." I thought, "Oh, no. Here is one more English phrase I have to learn."

My friend explained her meaning, and for a short while thereafter I was intrigued. "Falling out of grace. What a fascinating idea." But as I sat with it, I became increasingly uneasy, to the point that, eventually, I became upset. "Why would she suggest such a thing? That isn't me, is it? Could I have fallen out of grace, as she says, and not even be aware of it?"

In the days that followed, as I reflected on our conversation, it became evident to me that I had, indeed, fallen from grace. There was no doubt in my mind. I had done so in many dimensions of my world. The feeling of being out of grace was everywhere present in my life, and yet I had avoided finding words to describe it. Perhaps I believed, at some level, that as long as I did not put my situation into words, questions could remain, and I could look for answers to them later if they didn't just go away on their own.

The first such questions were raised in 1991, when I left my village in Burkina Faso and came to the West. Already I was trailing a huge elephant called "Failure." The simple fact of leaving behind the security and support of the village can be understood as a fall from grace. Life away from my community for more than a decade has also been a great challenge, and I have experienced many crashes. The collapse of an intimate relationship, and the loss of a brother and beloved uncle have been, perhaps, the most significant of these. Even now, as I complete this book, I am aware of how far I have fallen from the grace of my cultural roots. For many generations the wisdom of my village was preserved by a strictly oral tradition, and from this an encroaching world has persuaded me to break away.

I tell you, it can be easy to take comfort in believing that one's misfortunes are caused by others. I could blame the elders, sitting in the village thousands of miles away, who are unaware of, or do not understand my struggles in the West. But that would mean not healing, being a prisoner in my own trap, fearful of change. Instead I have taken refuge in the words of one of my wisest teachers: my grandmother. "Failure is the best thing that can happen to you," she once said.

I still remember when one of my brothers came back from school, upset and fearful because he had failed a grade. When the news got to Grandmother she said to him, "Is that what's worrying you? Well, if they cook a sauce and you do not like it, then cook something to your own taste." If my brother did not like what was being taught, she proposed, then he should put it aside and turn his energy toward the things that interested him.

When my brother's teachers heard this, they were offended, but for us children, it was not only funny (especially when said in Dagara), it was music to our ears. Grandmother's advice has stayed with me ever since, and has given me strength to find in failure the paths to growth I would have otherwise overlooked.

I realized the minute I decided to write this book that it would never be complete. We are in a continuous process of rebuilding ourselves, in ways unique to every situation, and so long as we live we are destined to fall again. In addition, there are more ways in which one can fall out of grace — and come back to it — than could ever fit within a book. You will find thoughts and stories here that are incomplete or unresolved. They, too, hold lessons, and this was the only way to write truthfully.

Failure will always exist, and the book that matters is written individually every day of our lives. My wish is that you will write it for yourself in a way that brings healing, wisdom and peace.

Sobonfu E. Somé
Sacramento, California

Falling Out of Grace
Meditations on Loss, Healing and Wisdom

Chapter One
The State of Grace

Let me begin by sharing some thoughts about the state of grace itself, about what people mean when they describe a person as living in a state of grace, and make a few observations about the expectation many people have that life will be, or ought to be, wonderful.

The state of grace is that holy and contented way of being that each of us strives for. It is that state, auspicious in the spiritual realm, in which we work out all our difficulties with care, and function peacefully in connection with other people in the flow of life. It involves progress in accomplishing the purpose for which we were born into the world in a way that is pleasing to those around us. It is a state of devotion and integrity, of living harmoniously, of being looked at not as someone who is perfect, but as someone that others trust and respect. It implies a certain level of healthiness and psychological well-being.

The state of grace is not the same as success in any measurable way, nor is it reflected in social status. It is not determined by how much we resemble those whom many people admire. In fact, the person who has arrived at this state may not even be conscious of it.

Each of us passes in and out of this state many times in our life. This is a universal human experience. As we fall out of grace it looks and feels to us as if we are failing. Indeed we call it "failure"; a part of us dies. But this is the process by which we make space for the birth of something new, something more true to ourselves.

Something needs to be broken in order for a new state of grace to be born. It is the natural cycle of our spirit. In this way we are born and die many times in life before we eventually return to the land of the ancestors. If we are going to achieve our purpose in life, we must be willing to fall out of grace and accept its lessons. When we feel righteous about ourselves, or deny our brokenness, we are fighting against the higher states of grace that await us.

Failure is built into grace. You cannot have one without the other. It's like two sides of a single coin. Everyone who has achieved a state of grace is certain at some point to fall, and to have fallen many times before. Every successful person, everyone you respect, will tell you that they have mountains of failure behind them.

Dealing with reversals is much easier in my village than it is here in the West. In the village you have people who are concerned about you and support you, knowing that their own happiness is dependent upon you. They also understand that failures are life-giving, that they are the engines of wisdom. Failures, they say there, come to show you that you are stagnant or wandering or that you have work to do.

Here is something I have been taught, and which I have had to learn over and over again through experience: To fall out of grace is a gift, one of the greatest gifts that one receives in life.

When we are in grace, we begin to take things for granted and we actually stop working on ourselves. Falling out of grace shakes us up. It reconnects us to the larger universe in order for us to see ourselves anew. It forces us to rediscover where our true center begins, and to learn what needs to be set aside.

Day-by-day we work to maintain our state of grace. We do so not only as individuals, but also as a part of several interconnected circles of support. When we fail, the work of coming back into grace is something we cannot accomplish by ourselves; it requires the participation of others.

The cosmos, the universe, is the largest circle to which we belong. This is the realm of Spirit, of goddesses and gods, of our ancestors. The next circle comprises the planet we live on, Earth. This is the place of air, water, fire, soil, stones and trees. Then comes our country and culture. Nearer to us is the circle of community, the friends and coworkers and others with whom we share our daily life. Our extended family makes up the next smaller circle, including our parents, children, brothers, sisters, uncles, and so forth. Lastly, I think of the circle of intimacy, which we share with a spouse or partner.

The role of all these different circles is to hold us in a certain place, in a certain way, so that we can flourish. When we are in a perfect state of grace all these rings are functioning to support us, and even if one of these rings fails us, as they always do at some point, we have the others helping us. Our well-being can continue. It is when several of these circles, especially those closest to us, start to break, that we experience a fall from grace. As they fall apart, we can be left feeling entirely alone and abandoned. We are no longer able to bring our gifts forward.

The struggles we experience at different stages of our lives are mechanisms built into us that help us rise to a better place. They are invitations to us to appreciate life, to appreciate the good things left behind, to acknowledge the sources of our disappointment, and then to let go altogether in order to come back to grace. They rekindle the acceptance of self, of others, of the past and present, and they offer us the animating experience of being welcomed home and re-embraced by the community.

For people in the village — and many other communities around the world for that matter — it is a given that as an individual falls out of grace, so will the other members of the community because of our reliance on each other. Indigenous communities also know that for the community to keep in touch with Spirit, this fall and rebirth of its members has to happen. Hence they push one another to take on new roles, to become adults, to become elders, or even to face death. They encourage each other to be swallowed by light, to let go of whatever comfort they are hanging on to and see that it is inadequate not to grow.

In the West, of course, it is so much different. Here the community will hardly ever support individuals who take a step off the cliff. To fall is disgraceful. There is, in fact, a fascination with suffering that is completely disconnected from the idea of growth. People do not see the goodness that grows out of failure. They immediately want to cut their connection with those who fall, and miss the point that the failures of others are also great teachers.

Knowing some of the rules of grace, for me at least, does not mean living with fewer struggles. I sometimes observe myself as an actress in a movie, and see that there is a part of me that does not really want to change. That is what happened when the elders asked me to leave the village and go to the West to share the ways of my people. I thought, "Wait a minute. I live so happily with everybody here. Why do I have to upset things? What is the point?" I crashed against the huge obstacle of my unwillingness to leave. Although I knew deep inside that it was necessary, I needed the community to push me, and to let me know that I either have to deliver my gifts or perish.

I wasn't sent to the West so that the village could be rid of me. In fact, I love the people there so much, and I thrive on their appreciation and the gifts I receive from them. However, it was necessary for me to leave this behind and be reborn in a new place, a place where I didn't know anybody, where my old world no longer existed for me. I would have never volunteered to do that. It was only the community's commitment to help me grow that made it possible for me to leave.

I have found that, in the West, the search for grace often takes the form of a search for ideals. "Who is ideal? Who is the best? How can I make myself like that person?" When the state of grace is understood as embodying an ideal, it can easily be turned into something distant and inaccessible.

In a world that has become individualized, fragmented and competitive, grace has become more of a challenge. When I think of how life once was in the village, I see there how community once existed in much of the world. People worked together at being in grace. It had nothing to do with being a leader, a hero or a role model. You didn't need to be the king or the healer. Whether you were the person who leads, or gives medicine, or cooks, or hunts, or paints, or whatever — each person had a position within the community where a state of grace could be lived. You can still see remnants of such wisdom in the names people chose for themselves, and which many of us have inherited: Carpenter, Hunter, Miller, Smith, Cook.

The idea, "Every man for himself," has a cost attached to it. No one can afford so high a price.

I think there is a kind of selfishness that is nurtured by the economic system of the West. In Western society there are so many opportunities for individuals to make big gains at the expense of the rest of the community. People will claim they have the right to do so. There are also certain religious dogmas that cause people to struggle with grace. Whatever religious tradition is dominant will affect the way you live, the way you think, the way you are judged. It's going to produce an umbrella of beliefs under which you are compelled to live whether you believe or not.

I have found in my work, for example, that where a certain, narrow kind of Christianity has been instilled, people accept that they have been born evil. This view infiltrates the way people look at each other. "We are all basically evil." The battle against our nature never ends. This belief automatically limits a person's abilities to come back into grace. It's as if one's wings have been clipped before she can fly. It takes people out of the state of grace in which all babies naturally arrive.

For some, the dance between what we truly feel and what we have been taught, between our natural purity and narrow-mindedness, becomes a challenge. Perhaps this is one reason why some people have difficulty being with children. Children remind them of how far they have wandered from their natural state of grace, and, perhaps, of the obstacles they carry inside if they are to enter into grace again.

Look at children when they're born. They are in a genuine place that exudes laughter, love, freedom and enlightenment. When you are with them, there is a vibration that makes everything peaceful. This is the state of grace where we all want to be — at one with everything, as a mystic might say — where there isn't separation, where there isn't confusion, and so forth.

The state of grace, of course, is not ours to hold on to so tightly. Life happens. We all grow up. Moving from child-hood to youth, from youth to adulthood, from adulthood to elderhood — each of these steps involves a kind of fall from which we have to rebuild ourselves.

Each of us has a stubborn conservative inside that steps out at times to stop us from progressing. You know, when everything seems to be working, why bother with all this stuff about growing?

In the meditations I record here, you will see that the fall from grace is a mechanism that teaches us to say yes to life. The stories are of regular people, people like those you know who strive to live life to its fullest. The struggles are real and the gains are permanent.

We are all like children learning to walk: When we fall, we get up, brush off, and start over. Every time it requires determination, learning, growing, transformation, flexibility and patience. These meditations suggest that the only way to remain in grace is not by learning to avoid failure, but by learning how to pull ourselves up after we fall.

Chapter Two
Close to Home: Grace and the Family

When I think of the challenge of grace within the family, a Dagara proverb comes to mind: "No matter how high a bird flies, it has to come back to Earth." No matter how far you isolate yourself, at some point you will always have to go back to your family.

To almost everyone, family is a delicate issue. It is a special source of love and pride, our original home in the world, and it can also be a source of pain and a ground for alienation. While some of us hold to our families with all our heart, others look for ways to break the seals that bind. It is fortunate that there is no such technology.

Each of us, you see, was born into a particular family because we brought with us something that we must give to that circle of people, something that they need — be it our gift of love, of labor, of trials, of joys. The experiences we bring to the family help it to hold together, to expand and grow in wisdom. The other members of our family, in turn, were born there in order to give something to us.

There is an invisible force that binds us to our family no matter what, a force that gives life. This close connection is, perhaps, why it is easier to fall out of grace with our family than it is in any other circle of life. Many things will push us out of grace with our family: issues of love, of money, of spiritual growth, of regard for ancestors, of choices we make in response to tragedy. All of these factors are related to our most basic human needs. Who, for example, does not need to be loved? Even rocks, in the Dagara view, need to be loved and treasured.

A friend once asked me after I had given a workshop, "Where can I go to find this loving family that you always talk about?"

My answer is that we cannot go looking for it. We cannot fantasize about an "ideal family" and seek it out, or imagine how some other family must be far better than our own. What is important is that we be willing to get down and scratch and dig and bring our own imperfect family back to grace. Because the truth of the matter is that each family comes with its own parasites, goodies, shortfalls, struggles and powers. Some families are spicier than others, and that's fine. Spice gives a family its identity, and creates the tools to bring it back into grace.

When there are problems within a family, it doesn't necessarily mean that it has fallen from grace. Family members can be in conflict and still continue to love and support each other.

Grace is lost when, for instance, people break away from the family because they are unwilling to work out difficulties, or when the family kills the spirit of an individual within it. It loses grace when secrets are kept, or when veils are pulled down to confuse people. Grace is also lost when one person is favored and others are treated differently, or when a family member turns her back when called upon to help.

I see some families in which the parents want to mold a child into what they wanted to be, rather than what the child was born to be. Whatever they wanted to do in life, or whatever they have failed at, they want their child to accomplish. It becomes difficult for the child, who was born with her own purpose. To try to live someone else's life is nearly impossible.

I know, for instance, a woman whose family wanted her to be a doctor. She felt obliged to follow their wishes. She was the pride of her family not only because she was bright and ambitious, but also because she was obedient. After she became a doctor, however, she wasn't fulfilled. She went through a series of personal crises, even as her practice was going well.

Eventually she realized that the cause was her career; medicine wasn't her calling. She resigned from her position and took up a less demanding job in a natural foods market. Her family considered this shameful, and so they cast her out. She had dishonored them. She took away from them the power of saying, "You know, our daughter is a doctor."

After several years of distance from her family the woman became a naturopath, very successful and happy. It wasn't until there was a crisis in her family that her parents finally began to accept her back and understand her choices. She had the opportunity to give her gift back to the family, showing them that being a naturopath was valuable. She did this by healing her nephew from a respiratory illness related to asthma that conventional medicine had no cure for.

Stories like my friend's are not very unusual. She chose to live and be true to herself by giving up her family's expectations. She fell from grace, and it was painful to herself and her family. But through this process the entire family was forced to grow into a higher and truer way of understanding.

When a child grows up and becomes independent, it opens the doorway for the second cutting of the umbilical cord. In so many cases the family falls from grace, is forced to grow, then reconciles. This is a pattern I see all over the world. This is part of the child's gift-giving to the family.

Another friend, who lived in Ouagadougou, the capital city of Burkina Faso, was persuaded by his mother to become a priest. For many years he was very unhappy, but whenever he talked about leaving the priesthood, his mother would say, "Oh, you are my only child and you promised me that you would be a priest," reminding him of a path he had imagined at the age of five. His father was no longer alive.

With this weight on his shoulders my friend lived a dismal life. He was unable to completely devote himself to his responsibilities as a priest, because it truly was not the purpose in life he was born to. When he could, he would avoid his duties and, as a result, he often faced the criticism of his colleagues as well as his mother. He was so deeply affected that at one point he nearly died, but every time he hinted at leaving the priesthood his mother fell into depression, calling him a reincarnation of the devil.

For a long time my friend's fall from grace had no clear solution. But eventually, after many years in fact, my friend found his true path. He reasoned that he was getting older and it would be too difficult to start over. He chose, however, to follow his passion for music, which he loved deeply and was able to combine with his duties as a priest. This is how he succeeded in coming back into grace, with his family, with his parish community and himself — by accepting his situation, discovering the elements there that fed his spirit, and devoting his best energy to them.

Finding one's true self brings learning and healing, but the road is often filled with suffering and wrong turns. In the West young people join gangs, experiment with sex or drugs, do destructive things, and so forth. In Africa, they reject village traditions, or leave the village and move to the city. My own view is that young people usually leave the village not because they will find a better life somewhere else, but because they are very naïve. Many come back only after they're sick, often with AIDS or with other mysterious ailments. Some come home to die. It is a fall from grace for the family, first to lose a child to the city, and then to lose them again to illness.

Some young people who leave the village for the city end up living their entire life away from home out of shame. What calls them to the city is curiosity about the material, the things that one can acquire. When they get to the city and find that they don't have what it takes for them to return home some-day with even so much as a bicycle, they're just too ashamed to go back. They find themselves out of grace because what-ever ambition made them leave was not fulfilled.

They stay in the city, sometimes for years and years. What eventually moves many to come back is the death of a parent. In recent years, thousands of people have also found their way home to villages in Burkina Faso as a result of the ethnic cleansing taking place in Ivory Coast. They return home for a funeral, or driven by the threat of death, and many of them find the fulfillment in life they were seeking back where they started, at home with family.

Like the naturopath whose story I related above, like the young people who leave the village — it is very often crises that bring about the restoration of grace. We come home through the back door.

I do not say that those who live far away from their family are out of grace. It is possible to be far apart and still be close by staying in contact and being present when we are needed. This is the shape of my own life. The distance that hurts us comes when we refuse to work on each other, or when we become intolerant or stop paying attention. This separation cannot be measured in miles.

Family members should be careful not to create situations where a parent or child falls into a state of disgrace and is stuck there. People sometimes make rules for others by which they are sure to fail. In the story of my friend the naturopath, for example, her family imposed failure upon her. They refused to see that she was growing into her purpose because they were attached to a mistaken ideal. In fact, their daughter worked very hard to please them, but their expectations were opposed to her life purpose. Her fall from grace was of their own making and, in a way, unreal.

Just as parents sometimes try to make children in their own image, children also try to change their parents. They sometimes fear being embarrassed by them. They can judge them quite harshly, even in the village. But there I think it's different. In the village a parent, especially a mother, is looked at as someone special, even though she may have many failings. There is an enduring kind of acceptance taught about a mother, particularly because she brought us into this world. The child is raised to be grateful for that, even if he has differences with her. I know I would always choose a place by my mother if everyone else were to fail me, in spite of all the terrible things I used to do to her as a child, and I know a place near her will always be there for me.

I have noticed that there are a lot of people who resent their mothers or their fathers for one reason or another and end up distancing themselves from their family. What they must not realize is that resentment devours a lot out of our precious energy and life force. Resentment is like making a cup of tea with poison in it for the other person. Somewhere along the line you always forget and drink it yourself.

When a family falls apart everyone suffers and a great deal of growth and forgiveness is needed to amend the situation. There are countless doorways to making peace. One thing that brings children back to their parents is having a baby, experiencing the birth process themselves.

Somehow, the mysterious process of pregnancy, of birthing, of becoming a mother or father, has a way of bringing new parents closer to their family. They see how difficult it is to raise a child. This helps them to have compassion for their own parents. It also creates a new role, that of grandparent, which is so important to every person in the family; discovering how important is another back door to grace.

A friend of mine who had an unhappy relationship with her

parents as a child became independent as soon as she could. She distanced herself from her family and didn't want to have any contact with them at all. In fact, she was mortified at the thought of communicating with her parents. If you so much as mentioned them, she would respond angrily. Sometimes she would even tell people that they had passed away. As time went on, her mother decided, "If that's how she's going to behave, I'll just disown her." So as much as they could, they lived as if they were not even related.

It was a very fiery and hate-ridden relationship, which they carried on until my friend became pregnant. After she gave birth she didn't tell her family, but they found out through another friend. They sent a card, asking if they could come and see their grandchild, but there was no answer until a few years later when my friend was worn down by the difficulties of being a single mother. She was forced by her crisis to let go of her resentment and pain. She was driven back into grace by her need for support, and by learning that the rules of being a parent are not so clear.

Even if our childhood was full of suffering and struggle, it does not mean that our parents should be denied the opportunity to try again. The next question might be, "What if they fail at being good grandparents?" My simple answer is, "This may not be their gift, but perhaps you can help them get better at it." You can do this first by accepting them as they are and not expecting them to produce miracles. We do not go to the desert and expect tropical rains. Then be there to help them find that something inside that will push the family through the door to grace. The birth of a grandchild has already opened it for you.

Some parents do not know any better. They are children raising children and may not be fully present, for many reasons. Still there is something sacred between parents and children that we must respect and use. We must always be careful not to pollute the rivers we drink from.

Our parents have held us in a sacred container, and to be able to go back to that place is medicine. I have, for instance, seen people literally sick with an illness that no one can cure. Diviners will tell them, "Look, there's nothing we can do for you. You have to go back to your home." Sure enough, they will recover just by going home, because there is some kind of energy that is very healing in your birthplace, or in your family's house, however hard it might be for people to see or understand. For Dagara people home is medicine. This is true everywhere in the world. Even in the West we talk about "homesickness."

How many people are sick without any apparent cause because they are carrying a family burden? A cousin of mine was one such person. He was very ill. At odd moments he would be overcome by pain. He had no control over it or relief from it. He lived in the capitol city of Burkina Faso, and went to all the doctors there. They couldn't find what was wrong with him. He went to several healers, and they, too, said, "No, we can't help you." He was desperate.

A diviner finally told him, "You have to go back to your family's house. Just go there. Spend some time there." He went for a month and, for some reason, the pain went away. He regained his health completely not because of medicine, but simply because he returned to his roots.

For me this story teaches how grace within the family is a whole different kind of thing than the grace one finds in other situations. It can determine everything else in our life. It has a power all its own. It is not the power of any individual in the family, but exists somewhere in the sacred space between family members, including ancestors.

In the West, I don't see that the culture prescribes any particular way of relating to parents and family. The common formula is: Be generous, be kind. But I don't see such a deep message telling people how important it is to honor their parents. What do we believe? That we can prosper without them? In Africa great emphasis is put on caring for family relationships. Distance from the family, tension between parents and brothers and sisters — it is apparent to everyone that these things will cause you to fall out of grace. If, for instance, you are having trouble in your work or in a marriage, elders will sometimes tell you that you can do all the rituals or whatever you want, but things are not going to work out so long as you are not at peace with your mother, so long as you're not at peace with your father. The lack of a connection in these relationships makes everything else fall apart.

A friend of mine who lived in the city of Ouagadougo had a fight with his mother over something small. His mother was living at his house and he made her leave. It was very hard on her, but he wouldn't consider any kind of resolution. He didn't want to talk to her; he didn't want any contact at all.

He had been very successful in his business — *very* successful. Then, out of the blue, everything started to fall apart. He lost clients, projects started to fail or get delayed, and so forth. His friends tried to help by referring people to him, but people would meet with him once and not go back again.

It got to the point where he started to think he was going mad, or that there was something wrong with him that manifested physically in a sign that read, "Run away from me!" He went to doctors who told him, "No. Your body is healthy. Your mind is sound. You don't seem depressed or confused." When I met him and he related his situation to me, I told him that maybe it was something that concerned his family.

He said, "You and your crazy ideas. This has nothing to do with them."

About two more years passed and then, one day, he was sitting in the marketplace in Ouagadougou waiting for someone. An old woman, a stranger, stopped in front of him and said, "You have been very successful, young man, but because of your mother you will lose everything."

He was kind of surprised and said, "What do you know about me? I don't have problems with my mother anymore."

"Don't debate me," the old woman said. "You have a problem with your mother, and unless you go and ask for forgiveness, nothing is going to work for you."

So he moaned and mumbled, and when I saw him again, he said to me, "You know, another crazy woman told me the same thing you did."

I said, "Well, just suppose there is a little bit of a chance that it is true, that maybe just doing this little thing is going to help you."

He said, "No."

Another year went past, and finally, things went so bad; his business came to a standstill. So one day he said to me, "Fine. I'm going to give it a try."

He went back to the village with a couple of his friends and his mother was, of course, surprised. She was so over-joyed to see him. She didn't even think about the past.

He said to her, "Look, I don't know what has been hap-pening, but I was told that I had to ask you for forgiveness. So if you would, please forgive me."

She did. A month later, my friend signed a big contract. When he told me, I said, "Well, do you believe?"

He said, "I still think it's such a silly idea."

I replied, "Don't say that or you're going to fall out of grace again."

Now I would not claim that all the problems in one's life can be traced back to one's family. I am saying it is always helpful to look at that area when we are faced with serious difficulties.

The consequences of falling out of grace within the family can be the hardest. Think about falling out of grace on your job: you can get another job; about falling out of grace with a friend: other friends will come forward. In the family, it's not like that. Your sister or your mother or your child can't fire you because the family relationship will still remain. This changes everything.

Even if you isolate yourself from your family the wounds of the separation remain. The invisible umbilical cord is still alive and it never stops pulling at you. There is no such thing as a one-person family; there is no one without roots. So far, no human being has fallen from the sky.

When we have rejected our family, it becomes easier for us to regard all the people we deal with as disposable. We lose the ability to send out roots anywhere. People who do this often end up tangled in shallow connections all around.

In my experience, many young people, when their family is not functioning well, will abandon it and go to a peer group, or, if that doesn't work, to some other realm — the world of the spirit, of art, of ideas, of activism — that they can feel a part of. They keep searching until they find an alternative support group that works for them. For many parents this process is a fall from grace. They suffer because they have failed to provide their child with what they need, and what the rest of the world can give them. At the same time, the child, too, falls out of grace by losing his family.

This process, which is so universal, has its good side. It

can force members of the family to reexamine themselves, to ask why they have failed each other, to reach out into the world and draw back to themselves what they need to bring the family together again. I have seen families where this has happened. It has enabled parents to open their borders, to embrace things in the world that they had not seen before. Also the child, in the long run, has realized that, even though he may be a part of the world, he can only arrive at his destinations in life by staying close to the nest that holds him so tightly.

Often a child falling out of grace with the family and establishing her identity through other communities will force the family to grow. Rather than seeking to pull the child back, the family may be moved to reach out, to expand, and to re-embrace the child, not by pulling her back, but by going out to her. In this way falling out of grace becomes the mechanism by which the family advances.

I was returning from Africa when I met an Indian family on my flight, traveling to America for the first time. Their daughter had been in the United States for three months, and then had decided to stay here and get married. They thought she was coming here for a short time, and now she comes home and says, "Hey, we're getting married." What was going on?

It was very interesting to see their resistance to this and, at the same time, to see their desire to see what is here on the other side of the world. They were fearful of losing their daughter to this stranger, but they were also intrigued by the fiancé, and by this country that was taking their daughter away. They talked about their fear and their excitement and they wondered, "Where will this unknown path take us?"

This marriage will certainly push the bride's family to open up. It will stretch the horizons of the family, and bring new challenges, new gifts and new medicine. Whether the parents accept their daughter's choice, or the fiancé, or her new home, makes no difference. The state of grace has been broken and they will have to grow.

So grace in the family is broken and restored, broken and restored, not by going back to the same place, but by growing.

Sometimes a family falls out of grace because it carries unresolved issues, spiritual responsibilities that have not been dealt with. These issues can be the cause of problems through many generations, and may end up injuring people within the family. When someone dies carrying them, they pass them on to their survivors.

I know, for example, a family that has been troubled by substance abuse. In this family's history, powerful spiritual gifts have been abandoned by certain ancestors, who chose to cut their connection with Spirit. Now their descendants are trying to recover these gifts through drugs.

In spiritual terms, addiction is a craving and a search for

Spirit. The addicted person is looking for a ritual, an initiation, a way to reconnect to Spirit. That connection feels like it comes through drugs, sex or alcohol, and sometimes these behaviors are fatal. This kind of destructive craving for Spirit can be passed on until the family's need for initiation is satisfied, and they are reconnected to Spirit.

In the Dagara tradition, we are taught that some people are born into families to serve as a janitor, as a humble person who will sweep clean their history. They carry the family burden, but they are also a bringer of light, illuminating dysfunction.

Many kinds of problem, they say, can be passed down through the family until they are disclosed in this way. Perhaps a great-great grandmother or grandfather has failed to do certain rituals. Perhaps a destructive energy is present. These things will affect the family in the form of some type of affliction, and the affliction indicates the need for healing.

It might also be that the family has a special gift that it has never put to use. In Africa today, for instance, you see many young people who follow the wrong path and get into trouble or get sick. When a healer traces it back to its causes, they will find a gift in the family, a gift for rituals or divining, for instance, that is being pushed to the side because the bearer of the gift no longer wants to be traditional.

I have seen in my village how, when a particular ritual is not carried out, people within a family can be affected. Let's say, for instance, that someone is supposed to do a ritual involving a water pot that feeds and cleanses his family's health and spirit. If the ritual is neglected, some other family member may have psychological problems or divisions may arise. If someone then simply goes to the pot and washes and attends to it, the troubles pass.

In many places, single-parent families are looked upon as a sign of a fall from grace. I see many single-parent families, however, that are strong — in part, because they don't fit the usual model. The parent works extra hard to make sure that all the things needed for raising the child are there. Whether that means going out for support from the community, from schools, from relatives, whatever, that single parent applies a lot of creative thinking and energy, which makes it possible for the child to experience life fully. In other families, where both parents are present, there's often not so much attention paid to this. It's assumed that we don't need to worry so much because, you know, "We're all here. Everything must be okay."

For someone who has been raised in an abusive home, finding grace within the family can seem like an impossible task. To do this they must go outside the family and look to the other circles, finding the comfort and strength there that should have come from the family. Only from a base of love, self-love and support can forgiveness come, and forgiveness is what clears the family's path to grace. Because the family flows so deeply inside us, this challenge can seem overwhelming. For many it is a lifelong journey.

The younger generation goes outside the family. It has to leave home, to follow a different career, to relate to members of the community that the family has never associated with. Rather than resolving the issue by waiting for the younger generation to come back home, the family can resolve the issue by reaching out. That young person who moves outside the circle is the agent for the family's growth.

At the same time there is a need to step backward as we step forward. It's a question of check and balance. Certain values need to be kept as others are thrown away. The wisdom of the elders needs to be maintained, for instance, even as the world progresses. Losing that would mean losing the foundation of the world.

There is wisdom and then there is stubbornness. There is faith and then there is procrastination. Because wisdom is there, it doesn't mean that there may not be a blind spot. That's where the younger generation comes in to say, "Hey, you know, I understand what you are saying. Would you look deeper? You don't seem to be helping us."

This allows the gap to be bridged. The elder steps into another generation, peeks into it and sees its reality, then makes amendments.

I know a girl who came from a very poor family. She was bright and attractive and her family made sure she was able to go to good schools. In college she met a wealthy young man, married him, left her family and disappeared for a long time.

One month her family needed a small amount of money to make ends meet. They wrote to her asking if she would be willing to lend them this money because they were really struggling. She didn't answer. They wrote again, and then sent a relative over to see her and this person was turned away. He was sent back very coldly with the message, "It is not my job to give away what I have. Don't look to me for help."

This treatment created a lot of confusion and conflict because everybody in the family had made sacrifices to help this daughter. Now that her parents were of an age that they couldn't work, and she was in her prime, she was not even willing to lend them money, which they would have been happy to pay back. Her mother died with a broken heart.

The day finally came when the daughter needed help. First she was having money problems, and then there was a fire that burned everything. When her family heard about the tragedy they went to see her in spite of all the things that had happened, and at that point she realized that no amount of wealth could replace them. She broke down in tears and asked her brother for forgiveness.

He said, "I would never turn my back on you. Our home is there for you whenever you need it."

She realized that her family would be there any time, even though her wealth and friends may or may not be.

Perhaps it was growing up so poor that made her afraid

to lose what she had. Perhaps it was a sense of shame about her parents' need. In her mind, these fears outweighed the responsibilities that go with a family's love. There's something else here, and that's the act of God that brought the family together and restored the state of grace. People do talk about the grace of God, you know.

Chapter Three
Reaching Out: Grace and the Community

A supportive community is as fundamental to the well-being of our spirit as a healthy mind or body. Our community is the place that welcomes and embraces us in the world. It demands of us care and commitment, and in exchange for this we receive a group of people who are there to praise us when we do well and help us when we falter. It is the space where we are validated, where we are seen and respected as who we are, instead of being admired or rejected according to the standards of a world of strangers. When we fall out of grace, the community makes our failure bearable.

Again and again we fall from grace, and then we heal with the support of those around us. As we live our lives, this is what creates and defines our community.

In the West, people usually form their community around work or school, a neighborhood or a church, among colleagues, and friends of friends, and other people they have met along the path of life. They find their place in this community based on the special qualities and gifts they have — their kindness, their generosity, their wealth, their intelligence, their sense of humor, their beauty, and so forth.

Then, over time, things happen. Everyone in the community, at some point, is certain to fall from grace. One person will go through a divorce, another will have personal problems or get sick, someone will lose their job or betray a friendship — you know, bad things will happen.

In the West, I see that the person in trouble is often reevaluated, and maybe excluded from the community. I want to say that it shouldn't be that way. When a person falls from grace in their community, the circle that has formed around him has a responsibility to put those kinds of issues aside. When someone has been accepted as a member of the community, he shouldn't be put to the test whenever things get difficult. You put aside the question of whether he is good enough, or "Is he as good as I am?" The community sets those things aside and steps in to help when help is needed.

Ideally, perhaps, falls from grace simply shouldn't occur within one's community. Once acceptance by the community is there, grace is there. A person is accepted no matter how she performs. Many of us, for example, are close to people who are, let's say, irresponsible. What they promise, they fail to deliver. They are late. They forget. They do things wrong. Why in the world would we keep such people in our community? We do so because they are included. Because we know how to love them.

I love the desert, you know, but I do not go into the desert looking for rain. I accept its dust and heat, and when it rains, I welcome it as a blessing.

Communities are built on friendships, on soul connections, and in the real world, some friendships break down. This sometimes happens, I think, because what we call friendships are something else.

There were two women. They spent a lot of time together, they went out together, they went to movies together, they had dinner together, they shared their stories. Then one of the women got very busy and they couldn't get together as often. The friendship was still there, she said, she just wasn't able to act on it.

Time passed, and the other person needed help — simple things. She needed, let's say, a ride somewhere. She needed to call and talk about things that were bothering her. She needed a companion and the other person wasn't there for her. There was a fall from grace.

I believe that in this case the fall out of grace took place early in the relationship, through dishonesty. A person wanted something at a certain point in time. On that day the energy was on and the next day it went off. "I'll call you when I need you." In spite of what she said and how she behaved, friendship was never there.

This story is common. Many friendships are based upon situations, and once the situation changes, the friendship ends. I've seen that happen many times; most of us, perhaps, are guilty. I see this as a condition of modern society. It has no problem with people who pose, and then hide away and fail to show up when they are needed.

When I go back to the village, I often sit down with my nieces and nephews and tell stories about my travels. They say to me, "You know, we are watching you to see how you deal with the changes that you go through as you leave Africa, go to the West and come back." As I hear this I have to acknowledge that there have been changes in me.

One of the most obvious is that I lose patience when I go home. Things there move very slowly. I want to schedule everything into a time slot and I want everything to happen just so. I watch myself be really pushy with people there — "You need to do this and you need to do that" — and not really let them do things in their own time. The elders wonder, "What's the hurry?" while my nieces and nephews say to me, "You know, we're watching and we're learning from you."

All of a sudden I realize again that as long as I'm part of that community I'm not just a person for myself. Who I am includes my nieces and nephews and friends and everyone else there. Remaining in grace with them requires that I not just pass through and make demands. I have to work on my notions of time, and everything else that keeps that community joined together.

One thing I haven't lost is the deep understanding that I am still a person from the village. Wherever I am, I don't try to behave like I'm not from Africa. I don't try to pretend that I'm "modern." This is really bewildering to my friends who have left the village. They can't understand why in the world I would live in the States and then come back and want to be with these "old people," as they call them, and not hang out with the people in the city. I tell them the reason why is that the community is necessary for my survival and well-being. What would I gain by pretending to be someone else? Whatever that is would be much less than what I would lose.

So there are a few general rules that help to keep me in a state of grace within the village community that I am usually so far away from:

The first is to recognize the community's importance to my health and spirit.

Another one is not to pretend to be someone I am not — to disown or dislike the community that shaped me.

I also need to continually check and adjust myself to make sure I am right with my community, rather than expect them to understand things my way. I have to open myself up to their needs and ways and keep relearning, "Oh yeah, that's the way we do things. This is the way this community operates." I have to respect that and behave in a way that works for everyone, not just myself.

Still I know I will keep falling from grace with my village. Over and over the community sees this, and then they reach out to bring me back again.

While our community is an essential source of support, it also presents many challenges. One challenge I have observed is that communities in the West sometimes want to put certain people on a pedestal, to make them larger than life.

Whether that person is a gifted teacher, a successful business person, a political figure, or whatever — the community sometimes comes to depend on an idealized view of him or her that is unreal.

This situation, although it is seductive, nearly always leads to a person's fall from grace. This is not surprising. A false image is an impossible burden, and when people fail to live up to it — as they must — others become disillusioned.

Putting people on a pedestal also creates a danger for the rest of the community. Those who are so greatly admired may become an excuse for others to put aside their own work, their own responsibilities toward holding the community in a state of grace. It's as if the presence of such a person gives others permission to not try as hard. They think, for example, "This person is such a great peacemaker, we don't have to deal with that issue ourselves anymore."

A lot of my energy is devoted to creating circles of people here in the West who will support each other, helping them to strengthen and hold that bond. My own desire to have community has been at the core of it, and for me, being able to have communities and connect them has been important for survival.

When I think about my friends in other parts of the country, I don't see them as separate from friends closer to home, and whenever somebody from far away comes to visit, I try to connect him or her with people so they can meet. I encourage them to open up and share feelings with one another. One thing this does is help people get away from the notion that their community is like a club.

People sometimes think of their community as being like a club, but there is a big difference. In a club, you can only join by showing others that you have something — money or talent or connections — that the club values. Also, clubs devote a lot of energy to keeping out those that don't fit in. The better they are at excluding certain people, the stronger they become.

Communities are the opposite. They are welcoming of all kinds of people. They respect every dimension of the lives of their members. They regard the gifts and weaknesses of their members as ways to grow. They get stronger as they become more diverse.

What about a person who clearly fails her community? This question often needs to be considered at the level of the larger group. This person may be an indicator that points to the cracks, weaknesses and shortfalls within the community. This is often the case with those who betray friendships, who hurt themselves, who hurt others. Signs showing their direction show up early, but are not tended to or taken care of. The issues they raise are sometimes repressed or neglected by the community because they are an inconvenience.

When I teach people in the West about African communities and the position of the elders, I notice that students equate being an elder to having power. Some people start imagining how they would use this power; others start thinking of how they would influence the people who have it. This happens all the time in my workshops, where we sometimes do a lot of role playing.

I find this fascinating to observe, but also sad. It demonstrates one way in which communities fall from grace. For some reason many people seek power over others. If they only knew what that really meant for the community and for themselves, I am sure they would follow a different course. They would take a million steps back. It is the hardest thing to hold power over ourselves with integrity, let alone anyone else.

There's a difference between being in a position of power and being in a position of responsibility. Elders in traditional communities do not take power; they take responsibility and empower others. This is one thing that helps maintain the grace of the community. When you go to a village you won't know who is an elder and who isn't, because people treat one another as equals. That is the basic ground rule.

There is also a difference between praise and admiration. For example, in Africa, if a singer from a particular village is very talented and goes on to become famous, people who don't know her will admire her. But in her community, where they know her, she is still a whole person, with strengths and weaknesses, and also a gift for singing. The community supports her by offering praise.

Praising has in it something sacred. It is the role of a community. Admiration is something different. It comes from a distance. It is partly blind. It gives you an ungrounded energy that separates you from who you really are.

In the village, even though you are praised for what you have done, you're still, in a way, an average person, maintained, like everyone else, as a part of the community. If you have done great things and you start to fall out of grace, people are not going to be shocked or lose faith. They're going to say to you, "Hey, watch out. Something is going on."

In some ways I would like to preserve the way people lived in the village when the elders held authority. Now I see too much there of what I see in the West. The younger generations no longer invest the kind of dignity and effort and energy in one another that the older ones did. So the state of grace is fading as people in the village encounter the New World. They are losing the kind of respect for others that they once had. Still, no matter where we are from, the memory is built into each of us that there is a state of grace that can only happen in community with others.

In the West there are so many different influences from outside over which the community has almost no control. The most obvious are television and movies and magazines and music — things that come from completely outside one's circle and become a huge part of people's lives. And it seems like it's easy here not to be accountable, because you can so easily walk into another community, another circle of people, another school, another job, another city, another whatever. I mean, you can just keep walking away all your life.

People's lives change so much and so fast: where we work, where we live, even who we are married to. As a result our community is always in transition. People come and go depending on circumstances. I call this "disposable community." We dispose of our loves, our colleagues and our neighborhood if we feel that they no longer serve our needs. It's like consumerism: When you don't like something, throw it away and try something else. In this way we avoid situations that change us and help us grow into a greater understanding of ourselves and life.

If you are so uncommitted, so mobile that you move from community to community, in a way there's never any falling out of grace. There's never any dealing with disappointment, because you're always escaping it. There are no ties, therefore we never learn who we are in the world of people. We end up as children in our dealings with others.

One needs, therefore, to make a commitment to our community. Then as one falls out of grace within that community, let's say by making mistakes, by mistreating people as one will sometimes do, one deals with it and learns from it — not by leaving the community, but by learning through it.

For many years I was a gateway through which people gained access to a certain person of prestige. I loved the company of these people, so I entertained often and thoroughly enjoyed helping them connect with one another. My sense of community here in the West expanded beyond my imagination. Because I had grown up with the notion of embracing anyone who treated me as a friend, it never occurred to me that I didn't matter as much to some of these people as they did to me.

One day my life began to fall apart. Almost before I was aware that anything had happened, I was faced with cold reactions from those around me. For some I was a nuisance. For others, I was nothing at all. Some people found ways to blame me for destroying their dream world and resented me for not being perfect. Some people would brush against me without a comment. Others would quickly turn their face to avoid eye contact. In those days I felt so small and pitiful that I thought even death would reject me. I stood like a candle at the mercy of the wind of other people's hurt feelings.

Well, there was some truth to my feelings of failure. I had failed my community and I knew it. I had to really dig deep within myself to find a reason to live. With the love, support and comfort of others, I survived. Many people in my situation do not survive. They die of abandonment or a broken heart, even as they continue to live.

I was brought back to grace by what I learned was my true community. I found strength in the people who remained by me and those who joined them at such a chaotic time. I redefined my community, or perhaps I should say it redefined itself for me. That, I suppose, was a lesson in another way of grace, the way it comes not only to those who deserve it, but also to those who need it.

When we fall out of grace in our community, there is a temptation to withdraw and blame others, or to punish ourselves. I think that at some point we must put blaming and guilt aside and accept that we are being initiated into something new.

Let us give gratitude for all that happens to us — especially for the hard things, for they are messengers of wisdom. Then we can loosen our grip on old ways and let our lives change. We need to let go even of those people and ways and things that we want dearly — in order for them to find their own way back to us, or for something better and more true to take their place.

In the West, when people think about their state of grace within the community, they often think about their reputation. "My reputation is the most important thing I have." People here will say that, and be very protective of it.

Still it's not hard to find people who are dishonest, let's say, or lazy — people who are irresponsible, or greedy or unfaithful. Even good people can have moments like that and will get a bad reputation. They will fall out of grace with their community.

Reputation is important in the village also. It is not regarded any differently there than it is here. But for a lot of young people in traditional communities, I see it is becoming less important, and it is sad to see. For instance, some of the younger people think it is okay to acquire things for themselves and not give back or share them with their community. They even think it is okay to get things in a dishonest way.

One example is the stealing of shrine items from the villages — masks and other artifacts that are placed at the altars — and selling them in the city. Was this happening a hundred years ago? Even five years ago this would almost never happen. Now when I go home I hear many of these outrageous stories.

People in indigenous communities are changing, and so is their system of values. It seems like everywhere in the world the quota of honesty has seriously diminished. The pressure to get more and to stamp things with our own name has spread like a disease. It is like a new form of colonizing that doesn't carry a flag. Honesty and integrity are thrown out the window. The new way of being in the world looks to me like a fall from grace.

It seems like there have always been people who committed crimes against others. In the village, however, until recently, it has been different. The settings that would drive people to do that kind of thing have not been there. If you did something that was not honest, you would face the people, because people have been completely attentive to caring for their community

The fact is that now some people no longer fit in the village. They don't feel that they are limited by village law. They are part of the village at a distance, and have accepted a more powerful system that allows them to do things for themselves first. The setting has changed. At what cost!

The teaching in the village has always been that you don't own the land. You only borrow it. And after you finish with it, then it goes back to Spirit again. There has never been a question of who has what, of ownership, of competing for who can own the most.

That tradition is quickly disappearing as the state takes land away from people and breaks it up into little parcels where you have to build according to the government standard. You have to build a certain kind of house on your property, and if you are not able to do that, then you lose the land. Those who rule want modern kinds of houses with heating, electricity, a tin roof, and stucco — no adobe.

Why does the government even care? Because they want progress in a modern style. Talk about a clash of communities! So young people in Africa either have to choose what kind of community to join, or they have to find a way to live in two communities at the same time.

I have come to understand that it was necessary for me, by leaving it behind, to fall out of grace in my indigenous community, and, after I arrived in the West, to fall again here, in order to deeply remake myself as an adult at home in both worlds.

I see myself standing at the threshold between the young and the old and between the indigenous and the modern. I honor my ancestors' wisdom, and at the same time I know how to maneuver in the contemporary world, with computers, flight schedules, faxes and traffic lights. They are both equally "me."

It is a dangerous time right now for indigenous societies, and I am like a compass to help my village see what direction our old systems can go. My goal is not to bring back Western ways to exchange for village ways. My goal is to try to find out what is fated to go and what shouldn't be lost. We know that eventually things are going to change, but where is the middle way? Wherever it is found, it must be a place where an embracing community holds together the world of each individual.

Chapter Four
Living Our Purpose: Grace and Work

In previous books and in workshops, I have written and talked a lot about purpose, how each child is born with a special gift to give to the world. In the village, where people are very conscious of this, the purpose of each person is known at their birth, and the work they do in life is shaped by this knowledge.

In the West, most people, I think, believe they bring purpose into life when they choose their profession, but these two things are not necessarily the same. In fact, my observation is that they rarely are. Most people lose touch with their purpose when they go to school, or later, when they select a career.

Those whose career reflects their life purpose never feel the desire to retire. Many of the jobs that people take, however, make them think, "I can't wait to finish this so I can live my own life."

When a child's purpose is identified at the beginning of his or her life, does this mean that she is less likely to fall out of grace when it comes to deciding how to live and to support herself? On the contrary, her purpose indicates clearly the place from which she will fall. Knowing your purpose is like getting a diploma that reads as follows: "This is your life project. You hereby qualify for more troubles, because we all know exactly what we should expect from you. Congratulations!"

The first thing most young people in the village experience is a resistance to whatever they are told they were born to do. I have had resistance myself. I never really liked what my purpose, "keeper of the rituals," involved. When I realized fully what I had to do I ran away from it. Oh, yes. I took off one million miles per hour trying to get away from it. It wasn't until I got sick, and became sicker and sicker, that I finally surrendered and decided to get on with my life. It was only then that I healed. Still today there are days when the desire to run becomes so strong that I need the support of something bigger, my family or community, to hold me in place.

Often, even when a person knows what she is supposed to do, she may not feel like doing it in the present moment. She may feel like pursuing a career that seems more glamorous or ambitious rather than following her purpose. She will push aside the things that she is here to give; dealing with purpose can be put off until later. The result is that she eventually falls out of grace.

But even as we fall out of grace with respect to our purpose we draw closer to it, because it calls to us, louder and louder. The more we distance ourselves from it, the more we lose our will, drive and energy, and we are forced to look for a way to find them again.

It has fascinated me to watch people in the West work so hard, through counseling and rituals, empowerment programs, and so forth, to discover their purpose. The amount of excitement and adrenaline that is committed to finding one's purpose is incredible. Then there is the reaction of the people who find it. Many are disappointed; they don't believe it's what they want to do.

A woman I met in Europe at a workshop, for example, was struggling hard to find her purpose. After a lot of work she finally found the key to the box that held her gift. The next time I visited, she told me she had found it, but I could see that she was very sensitive. She seemed to resist anyone who pushed her toward the path she had discovered. She learned that she was born to take care of other people, and she had hoped for something that would set her apart from the rest of the community, something more heroic. Taking care of others is, perhaps, more heroic than many of us think.

The desire to change our career can mean that we need to tend to the spirit of the self after being disconnected from it for so long. That's what I see in what people call "the midlife crisis."

Almost everybody knows how to survive in the West, how to pay their bills, but many people pay too little attention to their spiritual and social needs. Maybe families would be better off without all those things that two jobs pay for. Maybe they're better off moving more of their energy in a different direction.

Changes in the world around us can cause us to fall out of grace in our profession; it isn't only things that come from inside. Today, for example, we see more professional men than ever suddenly without work while their wives are on the rise in their careers. For many men it is a crisis. The more traditional they are, the more demeaning it can seem. There is a need, for us to create new, and more accurate, definitions of manliness. The world is forcing it upon us. That is where lessons are to be learned from this fall from grace.

What is the role of a man in this changing world, at home and at work? I don't have the answer, and certainly it will vary according to each person, society and family. I ask men who are working on this issue to remember that there is always more to the self than one's profession. What is your life about besides your job? What are your values? What is your purpose? Answer these questions and the choice of a profession will become clear.

When I first came to the U.S. and was taking classes in Michigan, my teacher said to me, "You're doing so well. Why don't you go to a career counselor? He can help you find out what kind of job to look for." So I went.

The career counselor had me fill out all these forms, and then he came up with suggestions as to what I should do. It was funny, because one of the things he suggested was that I become a mortician. I don't know what I wrote down that gave him that idea. I found it very bizarre. I mean, I might go crazy if I had to sit with dead people every day, the whole day.

I looked at his list and thought I to myself, "He gave me this whole list, but he never asked me what I want to do." I was really puzzled, puzzled that anyone would give me a list of jobs to take without asking me what I wanted to do.

It has occurred to me that maybe that's another reason why people in the West have trouble in their work. They can't really make up their minds about what they want to do. They go to a career counselor, or follow their parents' orders, or just go along. They study things in college that don't have any real meaning for them. Then they go on into adult life in the same way, without every figuring out what to do with the hours they have to live. If, in the middle of that, something goes wrong — you get fired, your company goes out of business, you get an awful new boss, you lose a client — you're lost. Nothing has any meaning.

What I'm trying to say here is that, yes, we may find ourselves confused and the job market is changing. But we should see these crises as an opportunity to stop to examine ourselves and see what things we really need to do, what things make meaning in our life. If we know what those things are, it will be clear what to do when our professional life turns sour.

❖ ❖ ❖

Over the past decade, I have seen more and more women being clear about what they really want and need. Their heart is calling them to certain places and they are listening.

When your heart is there, and your gifts are there, it is easy to give your best. When you strive at something that somebody else imposes, you eventually find yourself in the wrong place.

Many women I know didn't start working at a young age. They first raised a family. Then they looked at the ways they interact with the world before selecting a calling. Starting later in life has helped them. They entered their professions being clear about where their gifts are, about what they have to offer, and what to expect in return. They brought with them the fire that comes from knowing yourself, and if you don't have that fire you're probably going to get lost.

In the modern world, people devote so much of themselves to their work that it often becomes the most important space in their life in which to heal and grow.

I know, for example, a woman who had a strong desire to be a teacher. She chose to work with at-risk children, sixth graders who had failed in regular schools. She herself had experienced a difficult childhood, and she wanted to show these students a way to avoid going to the same places she had been. She had a gift for communicating with young people, for seeing their strengths and helping them develop their areas of weakness, and she was confident this would make her a good teacher and role model.

When she started, her classroom was filled with children who didn't respect adults, and some of her students had seriously abused the teachers they had before. Nobody thought they would change, but she was able to respect and understand them, and to work with them better than anyone expected.

Even though she was an excellent teacher in many ways, she made mistakes. She eventually had head-to-head collisions with some of the children. At one point a student assaulted her in front of the rest of the students. She got very angry and pushed him away. That was one incident.

Then there were situations where she would break into tears in front of the class out of frustration and grief. For this she was reprimanded. Her colleagues would say, "No, no. You can't do that," and gradually she fell out of grace with the other teachers, with the administration, and with her students.

She felt her failures so deeply that she began to think about leaving her job. Sometimes she thought for sure she would be fired. So when the school year ended, she packed up and went away. She traveled by herself for a while, then she did some meditation, went into therapy, read books, looking everywhere for answers. She discovered that she was still fighting battles inside with her family, that she was still suffering from the abuses of her childhood. She worked hard to come to terms with that history, then she decided to return to teaching. Even after all the mistakes she had made, she still had a deep desire to offer herself as a mother and mentor to these troubled children.

In her second attempt at teaching she was much more

successful. She had learned to channel her emotions and everyone noticed. She believed that she had achieved the state of grace she was looking for. Then people began to talk about what a good job she was doing. They saw that she had dealt with her struggles so well that they wanted her to accept a larger role. She was asked to become the principal of the school.

This, for her, was another crisis. She was afraid that she would lose the one-to-one connection with students that made it possible for her make a difference. She either had to say no to the promotion and disappoint her colleagues, or accept the promotion and lose touch with the children she loved.

After a great deal of soul-searching she decided to become the principal. From the start she never liked it, but she had to admit she was good at it. More students stayed in school and her reputation for fairness and understanding attracted excellent teachers. But she realized that, as she feared, her close contact with children was gone. As somebody who did not have children, she felt a deep sadness at not being with them and laughing with them, at being separated from them. This was another crisis for her. She had to turn again to others to figure out what to do.

She went out to her community, to her friends and family, and that was when I met her. I think what helped her most at that point was, first, looking so hard for answers and being patient. Second, she met several people who had a similar experience, people who had been promoted out of what they really wanted to do. They were able to show her how important it was to give all that she could.

The solution she found was to work at two different schools. At one she teaches in the evenings and works very closely with at-risk students, at the other she is the principal, the person in charge. She has learned to love both roles.

This woman's career path is like a chain of falls from grace, but she has been able to learn and grow from them. First her experience of a difficult childhood, which caused her decision to teach; then her failure as a teacher, which taught her to reflect upon her own wounds and care for students in a better way. Then her move out of the classroom, which showed she could ask more of herself. This chain of trials resembles that of many who are brave enough to learn from professional failure.

Many of us tend to invest all our energy in our work, to give our best to it. We really want to strive in that area and be successful, and it can be very exciting. That's the way it should be. But we need to be very careful, very conscious, because our career alone cannot support us. Our spirit also needs social life, family life, and so forth.

It is also necessary for the community to have their eye on people, to reach out to them, so that their work does not alienate them. Without that, the professional world can easily cause us to lose sight of what is dear to us.

I am thinking of a man in West Africa who was definitely a genius. As a young student everyone saw that he was brilliant.

He would get very bored in class, so they kept moving him ahead in school, skipping grades, until he graduated. Then he went to the most exclusive college in France. There he was an "A" student all the way through, and then he became a chemist. The top laboratories all offered him jobs, and he accepted the best one with the highest pay.

This man was devoured by his work. He had no social life and could not carry on a conversation outside his field of work, but he was promoted again and again. Then he was assigned a very difficult problem to solve. He threw himself into his work more than ever. He cut himself off from the small community he had and put all his energy into this one project until it was finished.

The story I am told is that he found the answer he was looking for, and he was seen as a hero. But at that point he broke down. He didn't know how to reach out to others. No one knew he was in trouble because he had kept them away. He just went crazy. By the time his family realized what was going on, he was living in the streets. They tried to bring him back home, but he was mentally sick, and violent, and they had to put him in an institution. He is there today.

This is a sad and unfortunate story, but it is one that exists everywhere. It is, perhaps, the worst case of a story that is quite familiar. Clearly, we need to balance our personal and community lives with our work. Our work is not our whole life, and it is not even the most important part of our life. Even if it is our true purpose, it is only one of many things we need to accomplish. Overdoing anything we do brings danger.

Some of the geniuses and very driven people I have known have an adult mind in doing their work, but socially and in caring for themselves they are still children. When they are very successful in their work, their community often fails to see how much they need to be taken care of. In the case of this man, his coworkers, friends and family were so impressed by his mind, so in awe of his gifts, that they were unable to see that he was falling apart. In their admiration of him, they lost track of him as a person.

Perhaps in these thoughts and stories I can find a few keys to the state of grace in our working lives.

One is to find a profession that expresses our truest purpose; another is to balance our career with the other dimensions of our lives; a third is, with the help of our community, to hold fast to our purpose in the face of the troubles that are sure to come.

Chapter Five
The Directions of Power:
Grace and Leadership

Because I am a teacher and often participate in workshops and other groups, I have had to reflect upon the nature of leadership. It is an area where many of us will, at some point, fall from grace, either as someone one who leads or as someone who follows.

One question I ask is, "How do we measure the quality of a leader?" My belief is that we do so not by how much she does for us, but by how much she is able to inspire us and guide us to invest our own energy wisely, by how much responsibility she is able to make us take for our own progress.

What we delegate to a leader, she will delegate back again and empower us to use it. She might say, "Okay, I will do this much, but you must help me out with the rest." In this way the limits of the leader become the strength of the community, where each person accepts their share of responsibility.

The principle of delegating power rather than taking power is essential for good leadership. The more power a leader accumulates, the less likely she is to be a good leader, and the more likely to fall from grace.

In the first place, a leader who accumulates too much power can leave her followers in a position of weakness that, in the end, they will not accept. Second, accumulating an excess of power will make you shorthanded because there is only so much one person can do. The responsibilities of power can actually consume the leader and prevent her from doing what needs to be done.

It is important then, to see, realistically, that other people must participate. If everybody else is standing still, the leader is obviously not leading them anywhere.

The Mossi of Burkina Faso have a saying: "A king is as good as the people he rules." If a leader is going to lead effectively, followers need to do their share. If we see a problem, rather than saying to our leaders, "Why can't you fix it?" we need to say to ourselves, "Here's an area where our help is needed."

Leaders become lightning rods for other people's energy. Just think, there are people sitting in rooms all around the country talking about the President of the United States. Imagine 150,000,000 people angry at you! People do that when they have given away their power. Delegating power to a leader is a way of running away from responsibility, of avoiding pain and effort by assigning it to someone else. If we fail, it's much easier if we can place the blame on someone else.

One thing I observe is that people sometimes — perhaps I should say "usually" — have a very clear idea of how a leader should appear: what she should look like, sound like, how she should dress, how she should act. When a leader lives up to these expectations, they respect her and can overlook her flaws. When a leader falls short of these expectations, they see many flaws and forget about her gifts. This makes it very hard for a leader to be an authentic person, and very easy for her to fall from grace.

I have seen people approach a leader, particularly in the community of spiritual teachers, as if they were perfect, almost as if they were divine. But a leader and a divine being are not the same thing, not even close. When someone looks for perfection in a leader, the leader can easily be confused and corrupted, and the student is sure to be disappointed.

We want our leaders to be superior so that we can give them our power. We don't want to give it away to someone who's inferior to us, or our equal. "What is the point of giving authority to somebody who is just like me?" We take them out of the world of the human and we deify them or we make them into machines. Then it is okay to invest our power in them.

Deities and machines. They are like two opposite poles, but each represents a certain kind of perfection. The machine is unemotional and runs without a hitch or surprise. The deity is all knowing and acts without error. Two very interesting models for those who want to lead, and both lead to a fall from grace.

In order to remain in grace with their leaders, those who follow need to let go of the notion that leaders should be superior to themselves. Leadership is a gift that certain people have. It's a skill just like painting or storytelling or haircutting or anything. Leadership is no more special than other gifts. It's just one more. All people have a gift. Leadership doesn't make people superior beings. It just makes them good at what they do — at leading.

What you see happening continuously among political figures, and sometimes at other levels of leadership, is distinctive personalities becoming more and more like each other. All their rough edges, their humanity and individuality, get sanded off.

Take someone like former U.S. president Bill Clinton: People attacked him, in part, because they imagined that he would be someone unlike themselves, someone less human and more ideal. This is how it is for many leaders.

And so our political leaders end up becoming like robots who are supposed to do exactly as we wish, walking straight ahead with great certainty and never looking sideways. When they show themselves in words and actions, it is clear that they have basically forgotten how to be fully human. Then we applaud. "He has made it!" But we don't really look at the other internal things that have happened within this person. They have been dehumanized.

It sometimes seems that we create who we want our leaders to be, which may have nothing at all to do with who they really are. We create this space that has to be filled. If it is filled well, then we accept them, and if not, then our leaders have fallen short. In fact, what the leader has fallen short of is something she may have had no role in creating

I am reminded of another national political figure, whom I happen to like. I have observed this person for several years, and also observed how people talk about him. I've seen how common it is for people to complain about him. "He's creative, but he has a short attention span. He's too liberal. He's too conservative. He doesn't have time for a lot of, you know, insignificant people. He's rude." There's a whole list of this politician's failures. Eventually I realized that people were always criticizing him for not measuring up to a model that he had no role in creating.

People would say, "He doesn't follow through." Well, that is his nature. It's not his gift. He's an idea person. He comes up with ideas, he tests the waters, and then he delegates. He goes on to the next thing. That's who he is. So he must be hearing this for thirty or forty years in public life, people saying he has failed because he isn't a certain way. But he doesn't make the claim that he is. It is other people's projection of him as a political leader that they're measuring him against, and from which he has fallen from grace.

For a leader who has fallen, regaining one's position may not be the best way to restore a state of grace. It can be simply reclaiming one's own power in one's own sphere, one's sanity and health. It can be simply rediscovering that there is a human being within, regaining one's purpose and vision of life, and seeing that no one can live in grace without the recognition of his or her humanness.

You could say that there are two different kinds of leader: the leader who strives to be herself and retain her genuine identity while helping those who follow her, bringing along her goodness and failures and exhibiting both; and the leader who figures out and imitates the model that people want to see, showing her good qualities and hiding her flaws, "having it all together," and so forth.

The first kind many people find frightening, partly, I think, because it suggests that no one can reach perfection. The second kind of leader is more appealing to our view of the world. But this second path is a deception from the beginning. As a human being it's hard to be flawless, isn't it?

Can a person establish leadership without hiding his imperfections? I think he must. This is not to say that he should announce every day, "I am an emotionally crippled person, but if you come to me I'll try to make you feel better." But he can, from the beginning, say that he is a person like the rest of us, who has had experiences of triumph and also of failure, and has a gift of learning from his experiences in such a way that he can guide others.

I have had people walk out of workshops I lead because I insist on being myself. They begin by believing that I am a saint, somehow different from themselves, and then the basic human relationship between one person, who happens to be in a position of leadership, and the rest of the group is forgotten. They do not allow me as a teacher to also be a human being and to show that I can play and grieve with them. At times it seems I am asked to be like a bird with its wings clipped. I can't fly when I can't be myself.

When a leader is on the path, she will carry with her all her pluses and minuses. In fact, part of the power she carries is in embracing all the places she has failed, all the mistakes she has made. From these mistakes she cooks healing and wisdom, and then she has something to offer her followers.

There are books that say businesses should encourage failure. Failures in this sense mean that people are making space to break new ground. For every failure, there are a certain number of successes, breakthroughs, new things, better things. It is similar in leadership, and every other part of life. If we think that failure is negative we avoid taking risks, and that is how we stagnate. Grace slips away and won't come back until we push ourselves again.

When leaders leave the place where they are able to fail, they lose their value as guides. They are no longer on the path of growth, the path of healing and wisdom, along which others had hoped to follow them.

Think of the family. Parents lead the household. They are responsible for taking care of things and for the raising of children. Early on, children understand that their parents aren't perfect, and yet parents are able to maintain their leadership role. The family can accommodate a very human definition of leadership quite naturally, whereas in other kinds of situations in life, people have unrealistic expectations.

Perhaps some people hope to do better than the kind of leadership that they had in the family when they were children. It's as if we resent that more human kind of leadership because it forces us to accept that we will always be imperfect, no matter how much we grow. Consequently we try to look for somebody outside our circle, whose story we don't really know, and we project perfection onto this person.

Leaders are just as much students as those who follow them. In fact, life for all of us is an eternal school. There is a Dagara saying: "Each person is a student. If you stop learning you must stop existing." Questions that followers bring to their leaders lead them to new places, where they find answers they didn't have before.

Many people accept the idea that life is like a competition. Competitive sports, especially among men, are looked at as a model of life, and people look for leaders who will help them "win."

But there is a big difference between games of sport and reality, between competition and real life. Life is growth; life means helping, and being helped by, everyone around us; life is an eternal force that brings increasing insight and wisdom — things which are outside the realm of competition.

And so, in our leaders, we need to put aside simplistic ideas about winning and losing, and find people who empower us to move forward in our lives.

Chapter Six
Perfecting Wisdom:
Grace and the Spiritual Path

There is true spirituality in every religious tradition. They all boil down to the same essence. It is the clothes we dress them in that make them appear to be different.

Spirituality is the path of wisdom within every religion and way of life that leads a person to growth and enlightenment. It looks beyond the physical and material into the soul without judgement. Spirituality is the foundation of our search for meaning, our way of connecting in a sacred manner to everything.

It is common for people to fall out of grace with the spiritual tradition they were born into. It happens in the West and it happens in Africa. My belief is that students need to reconcile with their spiritual roots before they can usefully look into other paths.

For the most part, the crisis that a person experiences with her own roots will lead to a general crisis with all the other traditions. However much she may want to embrace them — one of them or parts of them — something will stand between her and the new practices she is drawn to. So it is very important for us to know that, if we don't reconcile with our own tradition, if we don't do work in that area, we are simply running away. We will always return to the obstacle we faced before. The crisis we had will be transferred to the new tradition, making it impossible for us to grow spiritually through it.

If you are not in harmony, or in a certain state of grace, with your own spiritual tradition, it will be impossible for you to sincerely embrace a new one. You would be putting a mask over a deep crisis, and when that happens, every tradition will slip from your grasp. You will disrespect — not consciously, but out of confusion — every truth you reach for.

Let's just say that a student comes out of the Christian tradition who is unfulfilled, dissatisfied, and then she encounters Dagara spiritual teachings. Well, she can only go so far before she has to go back and make peace with where she has come from.

For this there are certain teachings and rituals that I do, which one might call "ancestral healing." This is a way to restore your state of grace with your ancestors, and with the tradition from which you come. Ancestral healing is very important — in fact, necessary — in bridging between the tradition from which you come to the new tradition you are trying to embrace. Without that bridge, there is an obstacle that stands in your way. The student must go back to her root tradition in order to heal.

Some of my students who were raised as Christians are disappointed to hear me say, "You have to stop and deal with this."

They say, "But I don't want to do that!"

I say, "Well, it is a necessary step. Isn't Jesus an ancestor?"

It is like a tree. You must allow yourself to take root in the tradition from which you come, to heal those wounds if they are there. Then, from that place, you can branch out and embrace what is new.

We fall out of grace not only when we run away from our roots, but also when we idealize our tradition and our spiritual path. By coming into contact with other traditions, we are able to clear up our spiritual blind spots in order to renew ourselves. It is the same with any group: When you are inbred for too long, you can be crippled. You need to bring in new energy in order to thrive.

When you look at the different countries in Africa, it's troubling. There is so much war. We often overlook the fact that the people of Africa who are fighting are no longer connected to their spiritual traditions, that they have completely abandoned them. Outside influences have made people ashamed of their own background. Then we wonder why they're having all these different problems.

I see it as being deeply related to the fact that they have

fallen from grace with respect to their own spiritual roots. They have tried to embrace a western tradition without any kind of foundation. As a result, they go crazy.

When you talk to these people about the spirituality of their ancestors, they will hold a hat over their head saying, "I don't want to hear it. I don't want to talk about it." They consider their own beliefs to be superstition.

Even though African countries have achieved "independence," their own spirituality is still very much imprisoned by the cultures that colonized them. It's an interesting dilemma to observe, especially in the people who try to run away from Africa and then go to so-called "modern" countries. They suffer a spiritual crisis, because the identity they have rejected comes back to haunt them. There is a lot of grief and sadness, as people fall out of grace with their own tradition and refuse to admit it.

"Christian by day; pagan by night."

If you go to the cities of Africa and you talk to people about village spirituality, they say, "Oh, no. These are not things that we do anymore. These are things of the past."

People will stick by this view until it becomes a matter of life and death. But at night, in the cities of Africa, go to the diviners. You will see people there, sitting, waiting in line to see the diviners, because they are no longer able to make any sense of their life. They are often surprised at what he tells them: "Go back to your village. There are certain rituals you need to do there. Otherwise, no matter what you do, nothing is going to be resolved."

The land on which they were born has a certain spiritual energy, and that spiritual energy is telling them, "I want to be in harmony with you in a certain way."

Until that point their response is, "No! It is too shameful for me to be associated with you." But then they see the only way to move forward is to step back.

In the Dagara tradition, Spirit brings the lessons of life through falls from grace. Crisis comes as the instigator of change; it takes you to somewhere new, where you find a higher meaning and purpose. If you are going to learn and grow, you can't just be stuck in a particular place. Crisis breaks you out and creates the space for Spirit to teach you. This breaking away from a place of stagnation, a place of comfort, and moving forward to a more perfect way is what we call a spiritual life.

When I think about how and why we fall in the spiritual realm, I call upon my own experience.

However crazy and scary this might sound to people who know me, I have sometimes seen myself as a capable student of Spirit. But then something happens, or I face some unknown situation, and again I see myself severely failing. No matter how hard I try, no matter how continuously I work at it, there always comes a time that I fall out of grace.

I think that's one of the reasons why I ended up being here in the West. My coming here was part of my spiritual education, and I have grown spiritually through a chain of falls from grace.

In the first place, I felt a lot of resentment at having to leave the village for a place so far away, a place I didn't really want to be. Then, when I got here, in a context where everything was so different from what I knew, I saw the West as a place where I would not learn anything. I became so resistant, so unwilling, that I refused to do the tasks I had come here to do. It took me a long time to realize that my reluctance to accept my destiny, to accept that Spirit was guiding me, was actually taking me to illness. I became quite sick. I couldn't eat. I was so weak.

Finally, one day, it was as if Spirit came to me and said, "Fine. Be miserable if you like. Die if you wish. But you are not going to get better until you accept that you are going to learn and grow by doing what you came here to do." It was only then that I started to feel better.

It was the stress of illness, I believe, that lead me to the wisdom I had been lacking. I mean, I was all but dead. I was down to bones. I couldn't do anything. I had this terrible stomach pain. Nothing could explain why I was sick until finally this light came and said, "Hey, if you want to remain in a place of resentment your pain will never stop. Know that. You have to continue to learn, to do your work, or you are not going to grow in Spirit." And then I got better.

Knowledge can only be transformed into wisdom through

experience. When a student seeks wisdom from a spiritual teacher, they are first given knowledge, and then certain experiences must follow in order to turn this into wisdom. Sometimes a teacher will create these experiences; sometimes they come naturally.

In parts of Africa, the spiritual teacher is there to initiate trouble. The teacher helps you by opening the doorway to trouble and helping you through what you find there. Sometimes she pushes you in, even when you are reluctant, because that is where you need to go in order to gain a piece of wisdom. Wisdom that is taught in a vacuum, that is memorized without being lived, is basically useless.

A simple example happened when I was five years old. I was deadly afraid of the dark — almost paralyzed, in fact, when left alone at night. When my female father (the first spiritual teacher assigned to a child in the village) heard about it, she took a lot of pleasure in sending me to run errands in the dark. My first assignment required that I walk about half a mile from my home. I was so filled with fear that a dog coming up behind me sent me back at a run, screaming. Everyone was worried that I had been attacked, but when I explained what happened they laughed so hard they couldn't stand up.

I was sent back out again with specific prayers, having faith that I would be protected this time. Then, after completing my errand, I enlisted a whole bunch of people to accompany me on my way back. After many assignments like this one, I arrived at a point where I had no more fear of the dark. Since then I have come to cherish the night time.

Some people might think this was abusive. I certainly thought so at the time. In retrospect I am grateful for the experience. Where I come from, day and night were equal. We lived without flashlights and electricity, and no adult could survive without certainty that Spirit will protect us from dangers we cannot see.

In every tradition I am aware of, to progress on the spiritual path one needs a guide. There are two ways of looking at this spiritual teacher. In the world of the Dagara, the teacher is understood as a messenger of Spirit, someone who nurtures the student and encourages her to embrace her own spirituality. He does that by sharing his knowledge of the spirit world, his experience, and by directing the student through different exercises and trials so that she might progress.

What I have observed in the West is something different. Here the spiritual teacher is, similarly, someone who opens the student's mind to what is possible. But the teacher is often expected to be a sort of divine person who can make the student divine, too, simply by telling her what he knows. It's a little bit like the way we have talked about the leader. The spiritual teacher in the West is often expected to embody an ideal that is more than human.

The teacher, like the leader, is likely to fall from grace when the role she is given, or that she accepts, is more than human.

This cripples the teacher. She is not free to be herself as long as there's a student around, not free to show any sign of pain, any sign of trouble, at all. And so she becomes unable to do what is asked of her.

I can give you a personal example. When people meet me, first, they see that I'm from Africa. I come from an indigenous community. I haven't had all these bad western, modern influences, they think, so I must have my act together. I talk about spirituality, so I must be this perfect person, someone to look up to. I always feel uneasy about this, and even when I tell people, "Look, I am not like that," people don't want to know about it. What they want to know is what they have to do to in order to be more like what they think I am.

Often, out of respect, I think, people treat me like someone who is helpless. I can't get up, for example, and go get my things. I am not supposed to have an earthy sense of humor, or show any sign of weakness, or have pain, or everyday problems. And I wonder, "Do these people know me? Their image of me has nothing to do with who I am."

These students want me to show them a person I could never pretend to be. If I did, it would not be true, and it would not help them to grow in the way they hope to. It would only trap us all in a false place and freeze us, so that spiritual growth is impossible.

The student approaches his teacher. "There is something inside of me, but I don't know how to access it. Is there anything you can do?"

Then the teacher becomes the locksmith. She crafts a

key, or sometimes she sees a key resting there on the student's neck. She says, "Here it is. Unlock the door. Now let's explore what is here. Let's see how you can use what you have found, for yourself and for others."

In Dagara culture, spiritual teachers are primarily elders. Elders are not seen as more perfect than anyone else. They are people who have lived longer, who have experienced things, who have lived and learned through experience, through observation, and so forth. It is not as if they have crossed some line and found perfection. Perhaps in the West, that's what many people are looking for in a spiritual teacher, and anything less isn't worth it.

But can we even say that Jesus had a perfect life? He lived through so many trials, and was rejected by a whole nation to the point of being killed. From the point of view of most of the people who knew about him, his enemies, he was continuously messing up. That doesn't mean that he didn't have wisdom to share. So it would be a limited perspective to imagine that because someone has wisdom, he will have some kind of serene life without any troubles. Jesus was worried about his apostles betraying him. When he was crucified, he had pain. So there's a humanity there.

That's what makes it juicy. Without the humanity, it would be a deadened spirituality, because spirituality has, at its core, something that is living, something that is based on experience, something that is based on our relationship with other beings, with other people, with the land, with the trees, and so forth. By virtue of those relationships, there's going to be friction, and we may not necessarily like it. We may not necessarily always be successful. So we take our frictions and failures, our falls from grace, and incorporate them into the fabric of our spiritual life. That is where all the juice comes from. Otherwise our wisdom is one empty, boring tale that nobody is interested in — neither the student nor the teacher.

We may think that since the spiritual teacher is not a divine being, or a divine-like being, then she is not a good teacher, that she does not have anything to teach. "If the teacher has had rough experiences, then she must not be good, otherwise how could she have gone through all of that?"

I have asked myself these same kinds of questions, as a student and as a teacher. "Why would I rely on a teacher who has had all these difficulties in her life?"

The answer is that, because the teacher walks along the same line the student is travelling — learning, growing and healing from her wounds — she is able to have the necessary closeness. She can zoom into the life of the student bringing with her the wisdom she needs to understand the feelings and difficulties and all the other experiences he is having.

Let's say, for instance, that you are having a lot of grief and you're going to talk to a teacher who has no experience of grief. She won't know how to help you in a very focused way because she doesn't really know what it is you feel. She will give you an intellectual explanation of what needs to happen that doesn't really satisfy your soul's desire to deal with this heavy burden. On the other hand, a spiritual teacher who knows the path on which the student is traveling will be able to shed light on the situation, so that grief can be transformed into wisdom.

In the Dagara tradition, if someone says they are perfect, then people will say, "Do you go to the bathroom?"

If he says, "Yes," then people will say, "Then you are not perfect, because perfect beings don't go to the bathroom."

That's a basic understanding. It makes room for the teacher, who is not perfect, to continue to gain wisdom through difficulties, through falls from grace, and for the student to learn from these trials.

Does the spiritual teacher have greater power than the student? No, she doesn't. The teacher has a special relationship to something the student is searching for, but that isn't power. I would say it is knowledge and the ability to transform knowledge into wisdom. If it is about power, I would say it is a key to the student's own power, the power that the student gains access to through knowledge.

The student needs to see that the power within is her own. If she refuses to accept this, she will eventually become helpless. Then any effort she makes becomes a waste of time, not only for the student, but also for the teacher. The student gets stuck. The student is unable to grow. As a result, it leads to nothing, until one of the parties wakes up.

Either the teacher is finally going to wake up and say, "Hey, it's time to learn or move on." Or the student is finally going to say, "You don't want me to grow, do you? Perhaps it's time to leave."

Time and again, I have seen people who wanted to be a spiritual teacher, but it's all about power. That is where you see the student and teacher fall from grace, because when you are a power hungry person, you don't want your students to grow. It's not in your interest for them to advance too far, so you beat their heads down as soon as they start to raise them. "You can't be any better than I am, because I am the one who is the one. Who are you to believe that you can be better than I?"

Unfortunately, power is often used by teachers to manipulate the student. When the student has denied that she has power, and denied that she has the potential for power, she and the teacher have fallen from grace.

There are situations, sometimes very public, where sex becomes a part of the issue. People are told, "If you want to move forward spiritually, this is a door, this is an initiation." People give their teacher the power to make that decision. Or people surrender their power to the point that they can be persuaded.

These are wrong departures. The student who accepts this situation has killed her ability to learn anything. At this point, even if there is no encounter, she has given away her power, so there is no way she could be learning. It's no longer a student-teacher relationship.

Often a student is in such awe of her teacher that she longs to melt together with him, to be one with him so that she can absorb his wisdom. If intention and boundaries are not clear, this longing can influence the student to initiate a sexual relationship.

Indeed, there is a powerful spiritual dimension to sexual intimacy, but between teacher and student it is not permissible. Both parties are disempowered and degraded. The student will learn something, but not what she set out to learn. She will have to come back to grace the hard way.

More often, I think, teachers are corrupted by money. In many villages in Africa, when you go to a diviner, if you only have a dime, that's what you pay. You put it down and they do the divination. If you just have a bucket of millet, then you give the diviner a bucket of millet. There is always an exchange between the parties (even though the amount is sometimes small), and the community sees to it that the diviner is supported.

In the West it is more complicated. There is a difference. When a diviner lives in the West he probably lives in the city, which is expensive. He lives without the support of a close community, and he does have to buy things — his food, his car. He has to pay rent. He has to get money somehow.

Another interesting thing about money is that, in the spiritual field, some people do not want to pay anything. They feel that if it's spirituality, you don't have to pay. It should be a one-way transaction. And I think that's what makes some teachers say, "I am going to have to charge more to those who understand that I need to be supported." The costs for living in the West are always going to be there.

So the complication of the spiritual teacher in the West about money is, what is fair? Can you expect people to be fair and to offer you what you need, or should you make some kind of demands? Part of my answer is that there always needs to be an exchange in order for the teacher to be successful. The value of his work must be represented by something given back. That is the traditional way.

Another part is that money is like power. There should be a balance of giving and receiving between the teacher and student, so that everyone gets where they need to go. In that sense, money is part of the issue of grace; it is one of the places where the world and Spirit touch, and from which the teacher or the student can fall.

Our spiritual teachers are messengers; they are not the message. In other words, they are aspiring gods and goddesses who have not yet achieved the perfection of wisdom. Our falls from grace show that we haven't achieved perfection either, but they are the paving stones of the path that leads us there.

Chapter Seven
Song of the Heart: Grace and Intimacy

Most people, when they think of falling out of grace, think first about intimate relationships. Almost every day I am confronted with these issues, whether it be personal, or whether it be through students, friends or family. Intimate relationships are an integral part of our life that we cannot escape from. They are the breath of our life and the heartbeat of every dimension of our being and soul.

At least I know that, for women, they are always at the center of the table. Never a day goes by without the subject coming up. "How are things going with so-and-so? This is what he did. What do you think?" So the phones are always ringing. The doorbells are always ringing. And we're always talking about relationships.

Intimacy is the language of the heart. It is the one song that everyone has in common. Nobody can say, "I never felt deeply about anyone or anything." That would be to deny something that is essential. Where there is no desire for intimacy, there is no deeper life.

It seems like no matter what we are doing, something is going to trigger in us thoughts of intimacy. These relationships keep us going. They are, for most of us, a focus, a center from which we relate to the rest of the world.

What ideas are to the mind, or what food is to the body — that is what intimate relationships are to our soul and spirit. People work on this every day in order to maintain their sanity, their tranquility. That's why we are always talking about intimacy.

The rules that determine a fall from grace within the intimate realm are blurry, far more complex than those of any other realm. Its source may be traced back to an initial fall from grace at our birth, or before birth to a parent or ancestor, and its ripple effects push out through all the dimensions of our life, which disguises its nature even further.

There is an excitement and, at the same time, there is always fear when we allow another person into our life. Intimacy requires that we open all the doors to our being and psyche.

When we bring in the spirit of another person we open up. We surrender to something outside the self. All our doors are open. That is a strange position for most people to be in: completely honest with another person, exposed to all the different elements that affect us, fully embracing the spirit of another person, just as they are.

The state of grace in a relationship involves absolute truthfulness between two people, between two things, or between a person and a thing, without fear of deception and with a certainty of acceptance. It means not only honesty with the other person, but also honesty with yourself. Otherwise, what is at work is not Spirit, but something else.

I think that today we are facing new dynamics; the shape of relationships in the world is shifting, at the communal and at the individual level. We are at a new doorway. Where is it going to lead us? No one knows for sure, certainly not I. What I do know is that the foundations of intimacy I knew in the old days have been shaken. In this kind of environment a fall out of grace, when intimacy feels like it has a double edge, cutting both ways, is impossible for most of us to avoid. What is important is how we choose to respond.

In an ideal world — a world which many of us imagine can

be true — partners would love each other and live happily ever after. Intimacy would come wrapped in all kind of delights and pleasures, our feelings would never be hurt, and life would be beautiful and painless. But there is more to intimacy than that. There is mystery, an unknown dimension to intimacy, which forces us to explore our depths. With wisdom and growth it brings suffering and healing. This is pleasure with pain in it.

Every intimate relationship involves the self, another person, the people who surround you, the place, and Spirit. The harmony that exists between all these different elements is critical in sustaining the state of grace. But even when all these elements work together favorably, you can be sure that you will still fall. This is what enables the relationship to grow. In fact, if nothing else does, the absence of growth itself will push you out of grace.

I sometimes feel that as we lose our sense of community and purpose, and as we lose our connection with the elders, the world of intimacy becomes more and more like a marketplace. Sometimes it looks to me almost like a job fair. The pressures that come from such an environment make people cautious and dishonest and everyone tiptoes around each other. This is a situation that many of us face, and we need to ask ourselves whether an intimate relationship is about sex, or money, or status.

In Africa, in the villages, intimacy is not about any of these things. It's about how two people relate to each other in a larger sense. People acknowledge each other first as Spirit, as Spirit with a purpose, then as Spirit in a human body. The connection begins at the soul and spirit level without turning the other person into sexual food.

We live in a world where many people have come to believe that sex will help them to create an intimate relationship. They will skip the step that brings in Spirit and just go to bed. What appears from the outside to be an intimate relationship is, in fact, a sexual relationship. In that kind of situation, two people can never restore the state of grace after a fall, because the spiritual foundation is not there.

I've talked to men and women here in the West who have problems being faithful. We all know how common that is. Sometimes they wonder about having an open relationship, with more than one partner.

In the village, and in many other cultures, polygamy is accepted. In other traditional African communities polygamy and polyandry are both okay. No one is bothered. A man can have more than one wife if his wife chooses to, and a woman can have more than one husband if her husband chooses to. The partner of the same sex has to be the one to bring in the other spouse.

What I see is that any of these arrangements has its own

set of problems. You know my mother often said, "I would have liked to have more women in our marriage," and my father, he would say, "Oh, no. I don't think I can deal with more than one wife."

My uncle has several wives, and the women live beautifully together. But sometimes he tends to be suspicious when he sees the women sitting together and talking. He's thinking, "They're probably plotting something against me."

He has developed this technique for dealing with their disagreements. He learned very fast not to say, "You are right, and you are wrong." If he made one person right, all seven wives would turn against him. "How dare you tell us who is right and who is wrong!"

Now he says to all of them, "You are right, you are right, you are right, and you are right." Then they have to sort things out, and he doesn't.

I imagine it has been difficult for my uncle to divide his attention between his wives. So having more than one partner may not be for everyone. I don't see that as an answer for people in the West for the time being. It's just a different model with different challenges.

One of the things that people have pointed out about my first book, *The Spirit of Intimacy*, and that kind of surprises them, is that it never mentions the phrase, "I love you." I think the word "love" occurs in it one time only. The surprise they feel comes from the fact that most people come from a place of show. Intimacy is not about show. It's not about how often you tell somebody, "I love you." When you love someone genuinely that person will see and feel it, even if you're not telling them, "I love you. I love you." They will know it. They will know that the gate of intimacy is open, and that love is not questionable.

People will use the word "love" when it does not come from the heart. It might be a wish, or it might be part of a seduction, but it is not the heart's word. To say it in this way is more torturous than keeping silent. Those who do so are certain, sooner or later, to fall out of grace and into the dangerous gap that lies between what was said and what was felt.

The words "I love you" can be like a drug that sedates people and keeps them from actually working on their state of grace within intimacy. When they hear them, it pokes them like a needle. They get their shot and then everything is smoothed out. They get thrown into this vortex where they are unable to walk to the peak of intimacy, to the place where sexuality becomes something sacred.

Our understanding of intimacy is challenged by the media, by the community, by friends, and other forces beyond our control. It's a continuous struggle between self and others, between the mind and the heart, and between the worldly and Spirit. There is a genuine craving to unite with Spirit, which

draws us to intimacy, but we are also moved by all these ad-
vertisements and songs and movies that show us what intimate relationships should look and feel like.

We are overwhelmed by images that make us feel, "Gosh!
I am not doing something right. My relationship is not as
good as that. Something must be wrong with it."

Even people around us will start to wonder, "What is
wrong with them?" when our relationship falls short of the
perfect ones we read about. We have to be careful of these
things, and not compare and analyze and fret over our relationships to the point of destroying them.

Realistically speaking, how much do our relationships
resemble those we see in the theater? A man says something to
a woman on a movie screen and he gets love. A man approaches
a woman in real life and says exactly the same thing and he
gets slapped.

We all still imagine Snow White and Cinderella and the other
"happily ever after" stories. But life is not "happily ever after."
Life is divided into mountains and valleys, and so forth. What
does it take to create happiness for a lifetime? The stories
don't say. They always end when the boy and girl fall in love or
when the girl is rescued. Those are the images we hang on to.
We don't get to see the rest of the story — the hard part.

And so in our own life, we look for a particular type of
person, a certain kind of feeling. Once we meet that person
and have that feeling, we think everything is supposed run
smoothly and nothing is supposed to ever disturb that. When
things begin to change, then we think, "Oh no, that wasn't

part of the deal. I was looking for someone else. It's time to move on."

But when the going gets tough it does not mean a relationship is dying. The rule is that old things need to pass away for new things to be born. And new things are pushing toward birth every day.

I like the way a friend of mine tells a story. She always says at the end, ". . . and they lived as they should." That is something we can all try to do, not live happily ever after, but live doing the best we can.

Someone might look for a relationship where there are no problems, no criticisms, and no disturbing elements. But that, if it exists anywhere, would be a mistake. It would mean the relationship isn't alive. It isn't moving forward and growing. I'm not saying you should deliberately try to find problems at every corner. You don't want to work at making your relationship hard. You want to work at making it purposeful, respectful, honest and grounded, so that when it becomes rocky, you have a space that both people will feel pulled back to.

It's not unusual for people in the West to say something like this: "My parents argued all the time. They had all kinds of problems together. I used to hate hearing them fight. But no matter how hard things got, they were determined to stay together, and out of that evolved love."

Another story goes like this: "The husband is very successful in his career and the wife is very successful in her career. They love each other very much, they never argue, they share everything, they travel together and they have a beautiful family."

I hear both these stories. Children want to be like the second couple and not the first, but I think that, actually, the first and second couples are usually not very different. What people show the world isn't necessarily who they are.

I've met couples that everyone thinks are perfect, and they tell me, in confidence, that, yes, they do have troubles. But they work them out in private, away from the kids, away from people. Sometimes they fight, sometimes they just talk it out, sometimes they walk away angry. The main thing is that they don't show their troubles to the world.

I mean, let's face it. It is impossible for two people to say, "We've lived fifty years together and never had trouble." That would that mean they have agreed to live together without sharing who they are.

A relationship can never be too grounded, but it can become too comfortable. This is sometimes a sign of people going to sleep, and not caring about each other and the relationship. They move out of a place of intimacy and into a place of the mundane, where they are living together because that is the easy pattern of things, while intimacy has actually died.

People have said to me, "I have become so uninterested

in my partner that now I'm just with him because it would be too hard for me to do anything else." They cultivate a sense of comfort with each other, but intimacy no longer exists.

When people are in that kind of place, they live outside the truth. Who wants to make things complicated? The door opens to outside spirits, energies and feelings that push a person to go out looking for spicier relationships.

You can say there are two kinds of comfort in a relationship. One is just a day-to-day feeling. "We didn't have any arguments today. We were able to get everything done and be very nice to each other, and we didn't get in each other's way." That's one level of comfort. But that's sort of a false comfort, because it doesn't really mean very much. You could say the same things about anybody, about the gardener.

The other kind of comfort is at the spirit level. It's at the level of connection where intimacy is, where you're really open and really participating with each other in a meaningful way. It's at that level, that foundation, that comfort really matters. You can maintain a peaceful household, but if that layer of true intimacy is ignored, the other level of comfort, on the surface, is just an illusion.

I knew a couple that had lived forty-three years together. As far as I knew, and everybody else knew, they were very happy together. When the husband retired, they decided to go on a cruise. For forty-three years they literally had spent very little time alone together, and after the cruise, the woman said, "All those years, I really thought the world of you. But having to deal with you these past two weeks — now I know that I really hate you."

On the cruise, they saw things they had never seen because the bond between them had always been so loose. They finally got to know each other. The man ended up going back to work because they couldn't bear each other's company.

I know many stories of couples who split up after being together for a long time, couples that seemed happy. We all do. I think in many of these cases there never was intimacy. The two people never faced the hard and sometimes painful work needed to build a relationship of love. Instead, they developed civilized ways of living with each other. It looked like love, but it was really good manners.

Do we want to be very civilized, or confrontational, or find a middle way? I think that finding a middle way is best. It's not about shutting down and concealing pain out of fear that you will make your partner uncomfortable. And it's not about living a drama where you pour out your emotions no matter how hurtful they might be. Both these paths get pretty sour and can spoil everything they touch.

Taking a middle way takes a lot of energy, a lot of time. A person has to stop and take care of their emotions, and then be very honest. Often it is just a matter of talking with your partner about what happened that day, about all the things that happened that affect how you feel. Sometimes it's not even your partner who drew out all that anger. It was something at work, or somebody at the grocery store. All those feelings are coming out at your partner. Walking a middle path means you have to be very truthful with yourself first, and then be willing to communicate where you are to your partner without being afraid.

I remember a conversation I had with an older woman here in the West. We were talking about relationships that break up. She told me, "If you love one another you can get through anything, unless another person comes along. If a third person comes along, even if you love each other, it can be very hard for a relationship to survive."

I agree with that only partially. In order for the third person to get in there, there has to be already an openness to the possibility of getting involved. Before the third person ever arrived, someone was not fully committed. The third person was just the excuse to cause a breakup. The state of grace was already failing.

Sometimes a partner's family or friends are the third party that enters the situation and undermines intimacy. There's a difference, but in this way it is the same: Whenever a threat arises in a relationship, a new and deeper state of grace is trying to be born, and both people must accept the process and all of its birth pains or the foundation for intimacy will break.

Someone once talked to me about a hard period she was going through in her relationship. "These ten people, they say we're not going to make it. I'm starting to avoid them, because it's going to be very hard for us to work things out if I keep being exposed to their energy, and we do want things to work out."

This experience is becoming more and more common. No feedback from friends can keep us blind, but bad tongues — *mauvaises langues,* as we say in Burkina — are deadly.

I know in my own life that has been the case. There were too many people, too many fingers, mouths and eyes not being helpful, but saying, "Something is wrong. Why is it this, and why is it that?" At times it felt as though some people would be happy to see my relationship fail, perhaps so that they might feel less hurt by their own failures.

So be careful. Some people will try to derail others who are in grace with their intimate life in order to find their own comfort. The social foundation that is supposed to help hold a relationship together can break apart, and then you are sure to crash like an aircraft with its nose down.

If you are committed to working things out, avoiding certain people is not the answer. Their bad energies will still come after you, but they will come from a blind side. You won't see them, you won't hear them, but they will creep into your house.

I believe, instead, that you have to tell these people directly what it is you want from them. "Are you willing to support me or not?" Let them know how their behavior is affecting your relationship with your partner, that *mauvaises langues* are a death sentence, and that they have to stop.

Now, if they say they are not going to, at least you know they oppose you — everybody knows — and they will have to be more cautious about directing poison at you and your partner. They know that their comments will be understood as coming from someone who has an agenda that is not your own. In this way you don't take on the burden of bad energy they want you to carry. They carry it themselves.

When grace is lost within intimacy the pathway back is hidden by great uncertainties. Many people begin to build defenses. They search out all their skeletons and carefully hunt through them for proofs that the relationship cannot survive. At the same time the desire to nurture the relationship keeps on arising and the heart inside cries out for help.

A couple needs to make sure that they are not their own enemy, that they do not stand in the way of a return to grace. Learning to get out of one's own way can be important.

I sometimes deal with couples who have broken up and want to get back together. They need to create a new place of intimacy within the relationship, but in order to do so they need to reestablish their trust, heal from their pain, and put aside judgements that they have made against one another.

In this situation I find it helpful to tell them that the process is not just about them. It's not just about changing and forgiving and being good. They also have to look at their surroundings, because even if they get back together, and they're still hearing and seeing little things that undermine them, the relationship is going to get poisoned again.

It can help them to heal if they focus on these outside issues before they resolve all the inner ones. I ask them, "How willing are you to hear bad things about your partner from your friends? When are you going to say, 'Stop. Enough is enough. I'm looking to you for support.'"

Sometimes when a couple turns their attention outward like this, toward problems they face as a couple in their community, they begin to restore their private intimacy. As they go out together and drive destructive elements away, they teach themselves to love each other.

When you're talking about the loss of an intimate relationship, you cannot come up with one formula that will restore everyone. You are dealing with things at the spirit level, at the emotional level, at levels where there is no logic. No matter what you do, you can't make Spirit or feelings behave according to hard logic. You have to look at each situation on its own, one at a time, in order to find doorways that will lead back toward wholeness.

It can be helpful for couples that have fallen out of grace to call to mind the intimacy they felt at certain moments together, even by travelling to places where they once connected, where they felt the genuine love they have for each other.

Most couples find that, in the beginning, they had rituals that carried a message of intimacy. There were certain things they did that brought them together, certain places they went. But there is a tendency to leave behind those rituals as people get busy with one thing or another.

For some couples, of course, the state of grace is never restored. They outgrow each other, or come into their own nature, or lose their purpose for being together. The soul of the relationship dies and they divorce, or move out, or walk away. All the bridges burn.

Coming back to grace then is an individual and very private journey. There is no universal secret potion that heals a broken heart. I have not yet learned such a ritual. Usually a person needs to go through a very, very slow, slow, slow process of healing. It's really hard, and it's hard to put into words.

For me, personally, trying to come back after separation has been a huge trial. No matter what I do, some people who have read *The Spirit of Intimacy* find my fall from grace impossible to accept. They placed me in an idealized position, even though I always said that I hadn't achieved the perfect relationship. They saw my husband and me holding together, and they felt that even though things might not be great in their own relationships, they ought to be strong and stay together, too. We were the model. So when things fell apart, a lot of people felt dismayed and betrayed.

There was so much anger toward me, a lot of rage, even from people I had never met. Still today I hear these incredible stories about how much pain people carry as a result of my fall from grace. I tell you, there are many days when I feel that too much of the world was placed on my shoulders.

My fall out of grace has also had repercussions on young people in my village, and across the whole tribe in Burkina. As a result, in addition to dealing with my own pain and my community here, I have had to walk this giant bridge of disappointment that goes from the West all the way to Africa.

The ending of my relationship has been a very difficult situation for me. I experienced one of the biggest deaths in my life. It was hardest when I went back to the village — it was like a funeral. People looked at me as though this huge, dreaded, awful-smelling corpse had finally arrived. Everyone was in shock. It has been an initiation into a new station in life.

The experience is not pleasant, but the pain and the harshness of it have been real teachers for me. One thing I have learned is to carry less on my shoulders, and to be careful to take care of myself as an individual, as well as my obligations to others.

I used to always talk about how I had never experienced depression and wondered what it would really feel like. Well, now I know! For three months I struggled along in a place of shock, and after that I simply could no longer function. I was totally exhausted and despairing. And did I say I had never felt panic attacks? Well, here they came.

You see, I've always lived in a context where I was in a relationship that defined me — with a sister, or brother, or mother, or father, or husband, or community. There has always been a relationship that kept me from being alone with myself for too long, as a person, as an individual. My first encounters with myself, I tell you, were worth several nightmares.

Then, after I allowed myself time to grieve and heal, I began to discover — almost as if for the first time — the things I like to do that strike a spark in me, things that I hadn't had time for, things like salsa dancing, like having time with myself to do whatever comes to mind.

I used to watch my sisters just pick up and go, but for me it had always been impossible. I had too many responsibilities. So changing in that way has been important to me in healing the disappointment, the anger, and the sense of betrayal from this crazy situation.

I have learned to be forever grateful for the changes that have come to me. I would never have made them on my own, but I know now that this experience has brought me to the deep realization that I am, and have always been, free. So are you. So is everyone.

What am I going to do next? Nothing other than be myself: Sobonfu.

I can't say there was any certain moment when something happened that changed my sadness and anger into peace with myself. I can't remember any turning point. It was a slow, inner process of grief through which I was able to rediscover and reclaim myself, with no magic moments. It was multilayered. It wasn't like I went to so-and-such place, or I read so-and-such book. It was a combination of big and small events, of receiving energies and finding support. It was a very, very slow process during which I kept myself pointed in the direction of healing. This, I have learned, is how it works.

I must admit I was an obstacle to myself in getting to a place where I could heal. In my mind I was a martyr, and I indulged in reliving my saga again and again. It wasn't until I learned to get out of my own way, to take responsibility for my past and my future, that I began to forgive everyone, including myself, and accept my situation. It was only then that things shifted. I knew I was beginning to heal when I started to be able to laugh at myself, and when certain little comments and events no longer hurt me.

Healing is always there waiting for you, and it comes when you are ready for it. You can't put a time frame onto it. You can begin the process, but its course will take you where it needs to take you. You just have to make yourself available to it.

For some of us, healing means going back to places and people that support and nurture our spirit. It means going back to the place of home and letting the spirit of the place take care of you.

For other it's about taking time away from home to reconnect with and care for the self.

For others it's about opening up to the community, and finding there a new way of looking at the world.

Whatever we do it's about reclaiming our spirit and power. It means asking hard questions: Who am I now? What is dear to my heart now? Where is my support system now, and where is my home? Our new strength lies where the answers to these questions carry us.

My healing has made it possible for me to think about my former partner not with anger, but positively, to give gratitude for the learning and good times of the past as I move forward. Now people seem to be surprised when I tell them that I don't have anything against him. If anything were to hurt him, I would hurt also. I don't have pain now, or anger. I don't feel all the different mixed emotions I did in the beginning.

I don't believe you can ever truly divorce someone one hundred percent. You will always have inside you memories of intimacy and the things that you did together. You will be drawn back to the past, for example, by comments from a friend who might say, "Remember when you used to do this?" After you have healed, you don't look back ranting and feeling disappointment. You feel again what was good.

People will see their own projection, their own disappointment, their own unhealed wounds in others who have fallen from grace in their relationships. Even after you have healed, they will say, "You must still feel grief that you're not telling me about. You couldn't have gotten over your feelings about your partner." We need to be careful not to let these people keep us stuck in the healing process so that it becomes an endless business.

There are people who will say, "Put it behind you. Forget it ever happened. Don't process it, don't analyze it, don't do any of that. Don't feed it all that energy. Move on with your life as if it never happened."

I know why they say that. The pain of looking into your fall from grace might be great, and for a lot of people there is a fear of creating a place of shame and doubt and self-flagellation. They will tend to beat themselves up. "If I had only done it this other way, then I wouldn't be here. I deserve to feel the way I feel."

At the same time, I know that when you don't address your situation at all, then you can carry away with you resentment and anger, as well as shame. These feelings are still there, and they will come out in your future relationships. You need to make yourself understand what happened so that you can learn, so that you don't just repeat the same experience over and over.

It's sort of like what I've said about spirituality. If you leave behind one spiritual tradition with resentment and step into a new path, hoping that will be the solution, it doesn't work. In the same way, the bitterness that you carry with you from a lost relationship doesn't go away. It affects any new situation, so you have to deal with it.

In the village we believe that spirits or ancestors sometimes play a huge role in making crises in the life of a couple. The spirit of an ancestor might show up in the relationship as a spiritual teacher and push buried wounds to the surface. The troubles this causes will not stop until that spirit has been dealt with. The ancestor's purpose is not to harm the couple. He finds out where they're stuck in terms of their spirit, in terms of their growth, and pushes them into that area so that their relationship can move to a higher place.

We also believe that some people enter into life already partnered by a spirit, a "genie." These can be male or female. Whenever these people get involved in an intimate relationship, it isn't going to work. In a sense, they are possessed, because there is this invisible spirit entity in their life that affects everyone who gets involved with them. One day their partner is happy, then suddenly, the next day, their partner will seem to go crazy over things that don't make any sense. Usually that means a genie is around, who can only be sent away through rituals.

A woman once said to me after the breakup of her relationship, "It's my fault. I am not lovable, beautiful or deserving."

I don't believe that anyone could say this truly. These words come through wounds, but only a beautiful heart can speak them.

Chapter Eight
The Fullness of Life:
Grace, Health and Mortality

When we encounter health crises and death we are reminded of our essence. By contemplating them we are able to see the fullness of life. Without them life and health would have no meaning.

Illness and death are natural parts of our journey, but society has evolved in such a way that there is hardly a place for them. It seems that we think of them as an exception, when, in fact, they are the rule. If we really understood that they were the rule, I think we would do things differently. The sick and dying, and the community around them, might discover the grace that comes through exchanging support and love.

Illness in the West is often a source of guilt. Some people eat healthy, take their vitamins every day, exercise, and do all the right things, and despite that their body gives up and goes downhill. Maybe it's a cold, maybe it's something chronic, maybe its cancer, or maybe it's a symptom of aging. They wonder, "What did I do to cause this?" and they feel guilty.

People also have a tendency to make others feel guilty about bad health. They won't say it, but they will think, "She must have done something wrong to be feeling this way." A lot of people who are ill and looking for support will receive this kind of response. Their friends and family will think, "If she were a better person this wouldn't be happening to her."

The guilt a sick person carries brings a lot of risk. People will choose not go to a doctor, or not to tell their friends, out of fear that they will be criticized. "Only bad people have illnesses." That is the idea. But if that were true, 100% of us would be bad, because everyone gets sick. I have never heard of anyone who never got sick.

So we are, each of us, called to be responsive to the processes of life that continually bring us face to face with illness and dying. Our first thought should be, "How can we help this person?"

The question is not, "What are they doing wrong?" It is, "Are they getting enough support? How are the environment and the world affecting them? How are the spirits around them affecting them?"

I never considered the connections between guilt and health until I came to the West. Shortly after I first arrived here, someone asked me, "Do you ever feel guilty?"

I said, "Guilt? What are you talking about, being guilty?"

It took me a long time to have a little bit of understanding of it, and I don't believe I have a complete understanding of it even now. However, I do know that when you feel guilty, you block the natural flow of energy inside yourself, and between different situations and things and people. Guilt has a kind of toxicity that makes it impossible for a person to heal, and, at the same time, makes it impossible for any difficulties you have in any area of life to be resolved.

People in the West talk about a mind-body connection. We know there is a powerful connection there. But one of the consequences of this is that when something goes wrong with a person's body, some people will think there must be something bad happening in that person's mind. "If their mind can keep them healthy, they must have failed to use it properly. Their suffering is probably their own fault."

With this belief, no one will see the grace that can be found in responding to the needs of the sick.

People say, "I have this powerful mind. If I knew how to use it right I would never have gotten sick," or "I would be able to heal." Often these thoughts bring about a crisis of self-criticism, which holds people in an energy that does not move. So one thing to remember is not to jump to conclusions. With illness there are many things that come into play.

There is the environment, and if it is poisonous you are not going to get well. There are causes from before birth, which, in the village, we call "ancestral inheritance," and the causes of these are out of a person's control.

We really must never judge the sick. Like every other fall from grace, their illness has something to teach us.

Many gifts that seem to be of no value, or even demeaning, are quite powerful. In the Dagara tradition, for example, people who are chronically ill are regarded as specially initiated. Their body has been taken over by something outside themselves, making them carriers of Spirit. Their body is a shrine, a gateway of healing. They show the community that something is wrong, that something requires care. They carry a message to the world: "Look at what you are doing. There is poison here. Are you paying attention?"

The situation of disabled people is related to this. They and the chronically ill among us show us the nature of our world. They come as representations of Spirit to point out problems. They remind us that something in the world is out of balance, and that we cannot reach true happiness unless we work to make things better for one another.

These messengers often do not feel their privilege. On the contrary, their condition can be felt as a burden and a source of shame. Their gift is not acknowledged or seen for what it is. We see power in our body when it meets the quota of perfection. Thus a person whose health is failing or who is handicapped is looked down upon. Perhaps the answer to this confusion lies in the ancient myths and stories where the sick and the suffering hold the power to heal and bless their communities. A shift of our lens toward praise and compassion would help us to see that such people are living their purpose, helping others to reach their own state of grace.

When we are young, we never want to arrive at old age. That's when we look decrepit and we don't want to look like that. This fear, and the fear of death in general, make us feel like we never want to grow old. And yet aging happens every day, to everyone. So I've always resisted this — the idea that youth and beauty are the same, and that the older you get the less beautiful you are.

In many cultures, including the Dagara, the idea is that you sculpt your face as you live, and each wrinkle shows a particular joy or pain you have survived. You would never have a facelift in order to look younger, or color your hair when it turns gray. That would be a loss of beauty, a loss of grace.

Some people feel disgraced by the fact that they are getting old, that they are going to die. "My God, the strength of my life is fading. How dare me!" They see themselves changing, and live in fear. They invest their energy in staying young and extending life, doing things that distract them from learning what life teaches.

Yes, it is important to do the things that help you stay healthy. At the same time I don't think we should attach any shame, any idea of a fall from grace, to the natural cycle of life. No one can say, "I will never die. I will never get old. These operations will keep me young forever."

Many of us believe that extending life is good. People are always working on this problem It's like death is bad. The longer you have to wait before you die, the better. But I'm not sure that's true.

At a certain point an elder will say, "I have used up the body as much as I can and I have seen everything I could possibly want to see in this world. Why should I worry about a few more years?"

Not long ago I found myself in a European airport, waiting for a connecting flight to Geneva. While I sat jetlagged at the gate, I noticed a woman, probably in her late thirties or early forties, sitting next to me and looking me over. I could tell she was puzzled by something and so I smiled. She took the opportunity to say to me, "I am sorry to be staring, but I am intrigued by your outfit. I can tell from your clothing that you are probably from Africa, but the combination with those boots is surprising." Clearly this woman wanted to talk.

I told her where I was from and why I was dressed so strangely, explaining that I had tried to dress for the weather. In return, she told me her entire life story in one fast sweep. The woman then stepped away for a few minutes, and when she returned she saw that I was writing. She asked what I was writing about. I told her I was thinking about my father and wanted to write him a poem. She thought that was charming until I told her that my father was dead. There was a silence, which, I thought, was meant to show her sympathy, but then I realized that our conversation had taken her to a strange and uncomfortable place. There was no space in her world for death, nor had she ever had a close encounter with it. She finally asked me, "Why would anyone want to write to the dead?"

After my flight was called and I had boarded my flight, I continued to think about this woman, wondering how she could have lived to her age without having an encounter with death. I am sure she, too, wondered about me. I realized that I had been raised in the village to understand that my life in the world is shaped by death, circumscribed by the fact that I and everyone I know will some day pass away from here. This awareness, I believe, helps me live more consciously, and drives me to explore my purpose and humanity. Without death, my life would be a journey empty of meaning and feeling. My experience and my relationships with others would have no value.

Death, in my tradition, means leaving this planet and being reborn in the world of Spirit, the other world. In order for death to occur here, birth must happen over there. So we grieve here in order to cut the umbilical cord into the next world. Without expressing those emotions we hold resentments and fears, we cling to images of the deceased person that are disturbing to the spirit of the dead and to the living.

We would be healthier if we made death part of our under-standing of life and didn't hide it. Some children, for instance, have lost parents or grandparents and were never told the truth. They were told, "They went on a trip." This is one reason why children grow up afraid of death. They can't even talk about it.

When I say that some people find death disgraceful, they sometimes tell me that's not true, or that's too strong a word — "disgraceful." But look at how death is hidden in modern culture. Old people are put out of sight with other old people and they stay there until they die. Death is made as invisible as possible in this culture, and so it is obviously a source of shame.

I think that most people would want to die at home. That is their ultimate request. Often that's all they desire: just to be able to die in a familiar place.

Death is like birth. Think about how you are born. When you're born, you don't fall out of the sky. Are you born in the middle of a highway? Should it be in a room full of people you'll never see again? In the same way, when you're leaving, you don't want to be in a strange place surrounded by strang-ers. You want to die in a place you know.

In the village a natural death happens at home, in the house where people live. It's very, very rare to see an old person die away from their home. To most people it would be a fall from grace.

When I was younger, my grandfather was ill and about to die. My uncle, who wanted desperately to save his father, no matter what the cost, took him to diviner after diviner. They all told him that death was imminent. Still unwilling to give up, he told my grandfather, "You have to go to the doctor."

My grandfather said, "No, no. It's my time to go. There's nothing more that can be done for me."

My uncle took him to a clinic anyway, and the doctor there said, "There's nothing that can be done here. He's about to die."

So my uncle put him in a hospital. He was definitely dying, and everybody was waiting for him to pass. Well, he wouldn't go. The doctors pronounced him dead several times, but each time he would wake up and look around and say, "When are you taking me home?"

It wasn't until they brought him back home that he said, "Okay. I have a few things to do. When I finish those things, I'm going to die."

For three days or so he didn't eat anything. I got up very early one morning and cooked something. I walked, oh, about fifteen miles to see him. I gave him the food and he ate it. Then he told me, "Just a few more days."

A few more days went by, and then he was gone.

So it's very, very rare for an elder, especially someone

from my grandfather's generation, to die away from their home. Even the young people, when they are dying abroad, they do everything they can to get home. They get on the train. Someone goes and gets them. It's only when they get to their land that they finally release their spirit.

Some people have a hard time dying. They have difficulties letting go because of their attachments to places, to loved ones. It's not easy.

It's like being born. Some births are easier than others. Some souls want to be here; they come right out even before it's time.

Other souls say, when it is time to die, "I don't want to go. I am not finished yet." It's often when somebody still has a lot to do over here, or has young children. Then they feel responsible for those children, which makes it very difficult for them to go.

For many years I had been told of cases where a dead person would cry. I thought my mothers were making this up until I attended the funeral of a young woman in the village who had passed away. After many years of marriage and trying to get pregnant, she had prayed to Spirit, promising that she would be good to any child she might bear. She had finally become pregnant and, although she had difficulties carrying the child, had given birth successfully.

She loved and lived for her child, and then, strangely, she

died, just one month after the birth, without any signs of illness. She cried her child's name until her last breath, and at the funeral we could still see tears falling down her cheek.

This is not a happy story, but it is true. I share it here to show how hard and mysterious the ways of grace can be.

There are ways to ease the steps of the dying into the other world. I call it "midwifing the dying." Midwifing the dying is a way of bringing grace to death. It brings comfort and assurance in leaving this world. Much has been written on this subject in other wisdom schools, and the Dagara people, too, have their tradition.

There are certain key elements to know in order to midwife a dying person. It is essential to know, for example, her purpose, her living spaces, her unresolved issues, her secret and sacred places, and the person that holds the key to her heart.

It is believed that a dying person relives her life in fast motion. She travels to places and people she knows to say good-bye, or in an attempt to reconcile differences they've had. This explains why so many people feel the presence of the deceased, or think about them vividly even before they know they are dead. They can make their presence known in distant places by a particular smell. It is not surprising to hear people in the Dagara tribe say, "I smell death."

When midwifing a dying person you need to have her in a familiar environment, and assure her that the journey back to Spirit is an honorable one. Then you have to understand the conditions that are holding the person here.

Let's say, for instance, that a dying person is separated from her home. It is not easy for her to die. She will continue to grasp at life until she has found a place she wants to leave from.

I remember the story of a lady in the village who was dying. In the process of midwifing her, people would get stuck. Everybody knew she was ready and that it was her time. She herself knew it was her time, but she could not make the transition.

People started to say aloud to her the names of familiar people and places to see her reaction. They eventually discovered her spirit was waiting in her garden. She had a garden that she loved, and her attachment to it was holding her there. They sent some people to the garden to call out, asking her spirit to come back to her at home. By the time the callers returned to the house, she had already passed.

When somebody passes it is necessary for people to come together to grieve. This is a way of cleansing family wounds and broken relationships. But I have seen in many cultures that grief is not accepted. When you lose someone dear, you are supposed to "tough it out," and when you do, everybody pats you on the back and says "Good job!"

That's like saying, "We know you have poison in your system, but hey, you did a good job of holding it in and keeping it quiet!"

The term "grief" scares most people in the modern world. They just see the tears and hear the crying. They don't see that grieving is necessary to heal at all the different levels of spirit and emotion.

In the village, there is the belief that when anyone passes, no matter what their place in the community, something valuable to everyone is lost. Every death affects every person. Everyone grieves together. One thing that is often overlooked in the West is the importance of collective grief. When a death is not grieved by the whole community together, it leaves the individuals who were closest to the deceased shattered and alone. They end up without a path back to the life of the group.

Grief is a language that goes straight through all the barriers to the heart and soul of anyone who hears it. We are afraid of people who grieve because we don't want to feel that. We have so many kinds of grief buried inside of us that we don't want to open that door. If we open it the dam might break, and if the dam breaks then all hell might break loose.

As a result, we usually want to comfort people who are grieving. "Don't feel bad. Everything is going to be all right." We want to sweep their feelings under the rug. But that only makes things worse. They will express their pain in other ways: through guilt, fear, depression, anger, frustration, aggression, and so forth.

That's how we train children to be good girls and good boys. "Don't show your emotions. Be strong." When someone passes, it is as if the person never existed in our life.

This is like saying, when you give birth to a child, "Don't cut the umbilical cord."

How can the mother and child live without cutting the umbilical cord? When someone dies, you also have to cut it. That is what grieving does.

We have trained ourselves numb and in that numbness there is much grief — grief so repressed that we don't know how to locate it.

In my grief work I find that many people are numb in this way. They don't know how to feel deeply because they have forgotten. It's not safe. As a result, we think this is the norm, that this is desirable.

And yet, underneath, everyone knows what it is to feel pain and loss and sadness. I have never seen anyone who looks at a person who is grieving and says, "I don't understand. Explain to me why that person needs to cry."

If you watch carefully, you will notice that whenever there is a major disaster somewhere in the world, people far away from what happened will break down and cry; others will start to speak harshly to one another, or get upset and fearful over everyday things. These are little signs of the huge amount of grief sitting inside people that they have not expressed.

The only time many of us allow ourselves to express grief is when it is triggered by popular symbols, things far away from our own lives, such as Princess Diana. Then we allow ourselves to express pain and sadness. Then it's safe. It's not part of our own lives or those of anyone near to us. This allows us to grieve without feeling threatened.

One thing I like to encourage people to do, no matter how serious the tensions are in their family, is to let go of differences when they deal with death. Death is an occasion to bring a family back together.

I have been to funerals where family members are not focused on the dead, but on those who are left behind. All the differences they have with one another grow larger. But I ask people to forget about that in the face of death and come together as a family. This is a time to direct your attention and conversation to the person who has passed. This effort of grief and celebration builds bridges between the living, as well as between the living and the dead.

I don't like the term "filling the void." Filling the void left by someone who has died means that you're not dealing with the situation.

There is a void. Don't fill it up too quickly. If you hurry to do so, you will fail to understand the significance of your loss.

"What has left my life? What am I going to miss? What

did this person really mean to me? How can I let go of the branches I'm holding? How do I stop the dreams that we had together?" These questions need to be answered in order to move forward with your life.

You want the void to remain there for awhile. Otherwise there is a process of training yourself to be numb, to not feel anything. You try to live your life as if the person never mattered.

Losing someone we love is an initiation. Our life changes. It is not going to be the same again. All our relations with other people and ourselves are forced to shift. We become a new person. Although a part of our heart breaks, the spirit of the departed remains. Through that spirit love continues to flow, helping to show us the way, if we allow it, to the higher states of grace and wisdom we were born to reach.

If reading this book has helped you
to understand, accept, and cherish your falls from grace,
then my goal has been achieved.
Do not hesitate to roll up your sleeves and deal with them.
Whatever needs to be done, do it at once,
for tomorrow may never come.
May the blessings of the Great Spirit brighten your journey.

Sobonfu Somé

Sobonfu Somé was born in the village of Dano, Burkina Faso, and came to the U.S. in 1991. She is the author of three books, including *Spirit of Intimacy: Ancient Teachings in the Ways of Relationships*, and *Welcoming Spirit Home: Ancient African Teachings to Celebrate Children and Community*. The founder of Ancestors Wisdom Spring, an organization dedicated to the preservation and sharing of indigenous wisdom, she is also involved in an ongoing project to provide water to the Dagara villages of West Africa.

One of the first and most widely-respected voices of African spirituality to come to the West, Sobonfu tours the U.S. and Europe often, offering training programs, presentations and workshops. For more information about her work, please write to:

Ancestors Wisdom Spring,
5960 Southland Park Drive #200
Sacramento, California 95822

sobonfu@sobonfu.com
www.sobonfu.com